SEVEN DAYS with *His Love* WITHIN

JENNIFER A. IZEKOR

ILLUSTRATED BY LIANE WILSON

 Zaccmedia

Published by Zaccmedia
www.zaccmedia.com
info@zaccmedia.com

Published March 2016

ISBN: 978-1-911211-06-8

British Library Cataloguing-in-Publication Data
A catalogue record for this book is available from the British Library.

For Tiajna, that you may always know His truth and love and that His joy will be your strength
Always

Contents

Acknowledgements

Proverbs 3:5–6 says:

Trust in the Lord with all your heart
And do not lean on your own understanding.
In all your ways acknowledge Him,
And He will make your paths straight.

IN THIS AND IN all things I acknowledge His Kingship in my life and I give Him thanks and praise for choosing to share these words and the Word with me.

For my daughter and my family, particularly the little ones... you are all that is, in and with Him. For my beloved K, it is my heartfelt prayer that you discover again the One who calms the storms.

Thank you, Liane Wilson, for the amazing Holy Spirit-inspired artwork. You have no idea how it encouraged me on this journey.

To Ian and Chris King, you bless me in so many ways.

To all my sisters in Him, Women By The Well Sisters, fresh from an encounter with the Saviour of the world... your love inspires me... thank you, particularly Sharon, Debbie and Isis.C and Pauline.

For Mum, I honour and love you

Finally Zaccmedia (Paul Stanier) for making this part of the journey so easy and carrying His grace in the process – Thank you.

Foreword

MARY OF BETHANY has always been one of our heroes from the Bible. I think it is because she "gets" who Jesus is when those around her are still struggling to work it out. We also love the fact that she is a "heart" person, in that her response to Jesus – whether it is in breaking the family alabaster vase and using its contents to anoint Jesus' feet or leaving her sister with the domestic duties so she can sit at Jesus' feet – is always that of a passionate, heart-led worshipper, willing to breakthrough cultural norms and express her love for Jesus.

We have known Jennifer Izekor for over 10 years, the time that she has been a member of Restore Community Church. Over this time, it has been exciting and encouraging to see the remarkable transformation that Jesus has brought within her life. As this book so clearly articulates, Jennifer has, and continues to be, on a journey from being primarily Martha-shaped, to now resembling much more of a Mary figure. As a person, Jennifer is well-qualified, very capable and has proven to be a real overcomer. All these, though, so easily can point to strong natural characteristics – capability, resourcefulness, a strong leadership gifting. Yet, as she has journeyed with Jesus, she has experienced a deep, inner change, where she has allowed any tendencies to self-reliance, independence and pride to be dismantled and replaced by real humility, a genuine compassion for the vulnerable and marginalized, and an honest faith grounded in the frequent muddy waters of everyday life. With this transformation, Jennifer's life has become a well of rich, pure living water that has become a place for many to find refreshment, whether in her immediate local context, or wider afield through her *His Love Within* ministry on Facebook and her *Women By The Well* ministry.

In Biblical thought, two words are frequently used for God's word – *logos*, which represents the over-arching word of God, and *rhema*, that is much more of a now word from God, that demands attention in this moment. Reading this book, Jennifer writes it very much from a *rhema* perspective – she writes what she personally experienced God speak to her through the Holy Spirit. As a result, it is not primarily an intellectual read, but rather insights to be savoured – that benefit from reading in a quiet place, with time to mull over, reflect and listen to what the Holy Spirit might want to say into our lives through His and Jennifer's words. Given that it is a book about Jennifer's journey from being a Martha to becoming a Mary, that seems highly appropriate. We are sure you will be challenged and inspired by the contents that you are about to read.

Ian and Christine King
Church Leaders,
Restore Community Church
Loughton, Essex London

Introduction: A 'Martha Place'

I was being 'Martha'. I am 'Martha', though not by name; I have become 'Martha' by nature. I am simply described by my Lord Jesus Christ in the book of Luke, chapter 10, verses 38 to 42 as if He were sitting right beside me, even now observing my frantic fretting: *'Martha, Martha, you are worried and bothered about so many things; but only one thing is necessary, for Mary has chosen the good part, which shall not be taken away from her.'*

It is a quiet, gentle admonition from a loving Saviour who knows exactly who I am and what I am doing! He knows each time I move into my 'Martha place'. He knows when I am seated in this place, where worry, fear and stress leave me living as if His promises for me and in me are nothing but empty broken shells.

I have heard His voice many times in my spirit as I find myself distracted from sitting at His feet, as I stray like a lone sheep away from His comforting and safe side. Like Martha, stressed and preoccupied with the business of 'busyness', I find another chore that needs to be done, another conversation that needs to be had, another problem to solve in my own strength, another mountain to contemplate, another wave to try to escape from!

There are many things I am not good at, but I am good at being Martha. I have developed my own routine, my own busy habits that keep me from His presence and the fullness of His abundant joy. This place has become too familiar, too comfortable.

He is here too, in this place right beside me. As in the biblical story, He has come to stay, to abide with me. He is seated here in my cluttered sitting room, patiently amidst the unpacked boxes and hurriedly stored junk. I should be at His feet; I should be bathing His wounded feet with my tears and drying them with my hair, in total gratitude for all He has done for me, filled with complete faith in all He can do for me if I just believe. Yet I am too busy worrying, fretting, afraid of today, terrified by tomorrow!

This place, this Martha place, is a place of disobedience to the Lord. Here, I live in disobedience to His teaching, His commandment, that says so clearly: *'But seek first His kingdom and His righteousness, and all these things will be added to you. So do not worry about tomorrow; for tomorrow will care for itself. Each day has enough trouble of its own'* (Matthew 6:33–34).

I am worrying about today, tomorrow and the days thereafter. I have become locked in this space and cannot find my way out.

Beginnings

T WAS THE BEGINNING of July 2015 and I was truly finding that each day had trouble of its own, and some! My spirit was troubled within me; peace eluded me, no matter how many times I opened the Word and buried my distracted eyes in Scripture passages. The walls of my Martha place were closing in on me and in the darkness I felt lost and alone.

I came to my Father that evening in prayer knowing that there was only one place I longed to be. My soul felt dry and thirsty and the first verse from Psalm 42, 'As the deer pants for the water ... So my soul pants for You, O God' was not far from my weary mind. Then I heard His voice, soft and tender in the night: 'My child, come, sit with Me... lay down your worries, your fears, list them all before Me, and spend the next seven days at my feet, and I will tell you of the thing that matters.'

It was an offer I could not refuse. I didn't fast for seven days, I didn't lock myself away... there was no striving or effort on my part, except to seek His face in faith and listen in wonder and obedience as the Holy Spirit, once again, gently opened up Scripture to me. I was watered and fed, I was led beside still waters, I fed in green pastures. Each morning as I woke I was given a new word and I worked my way through Scriptures, led as if on a treasure hunt to unearth new connections, new meanings and new applications for my life. In love and grace was I given; free grace with no end, and freely did I receive. Paul says in Ephesians 2:8–10:

> *For by grace you have been saved through faith; and that not of yourselves, it is the gift of God; not as a result of works,*

so that no one may boast. For we are His workmanship, created in Christ Jesus for good works, which God prepared beforehand so that we would walk in them.

As was my custom, I kept a diary and journal each day, and on day five, my Father asked me to share these words with others. A few months before, I had started a Facebook blog, 'His Love Within', aimed at sharing His love with others across the globe. It had grown to over 20,000 followers and I considered sharing these messages there, but my Father wanted me to do this differently. We both wanted this to be widely accessible to others, and so finally I had the material for the book I have always wanted to write.

In his book *Dreaming With God*, Bill Johnson says someone once told him "You know you have heard from God whenever you have an idea that's better than you could think up yourself."[1] The idea of developing this as an eBook was His and I cannot take credit for it, neither can I boast of the words therein. If I have anything to say, it would be to apologise in advance for not finding the words to express the beauty of His majesty; words are so limiting... but He knows He has my heart, and I hope that as you read, my heart speaks to your heart in a language developed by His heart. We are all one in Him.

I will not proceed to tell you how to read this book, but suggest that you read each chapter a day at a time. You may decide to spend a couple of days working through a single chapter as some are longer than others, but whatever you do, do not hurry through it. Take one lesson at a time and let each one act as a doorway to a personal conversation you enter into with the Holy Spirit, who is just waiting by your side to take you on your unique journey with Him. I am still on that journey and it changes every day. Enjoy...

In love
Jennifer Izekor

---

1   Bill Johnson, *Dreaming with God* (Shippensburg, PA: Destiny Image, 2006).

DAY 1 'Be still, and know that I am God'[2]

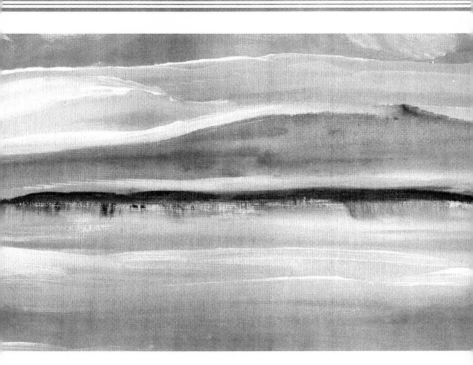

I N THE NASB TRANSLATION, this scripture actually reads, *'Cease striving and know that I am God; I will be exalted among the nations, I will be exalted in the earth.' The LORD of hosts is with us; The God of Jacob is our stronghold. ...'* (Psalm 46:10–11)

It is a beautiful verse, but one that I think is even more heart and soul-nourishing when read in the context of the entire psalm:

> *God is our refuge and strength,*
> *A very present help in trouble.*
> *Therefore we will not fear, though the earth should change*

2   Psalm 46:10, NIV UK 2011.

And though the mountains slip into the heart of the sea;
Though its waters roar and foam,
Though the mountains quake at its swelling pride. ...
There is a river whose streams make glad the city of God,
The holy dwelling places of the Most High.
God is in the midst of her, she will not be moved;
God will help her when morning dawns.
The nations made uproar, the kingdoms tottered;
He raised His voice, the earth melted.
The LORD of hosts is with us;
The God of Jacob is our stronghold. ...
Come; behold the works of the LORD,
Who has wrought desolations in the earth.
He makes wars to cease to the end of the earth;
He breaks the bow and cuts the spear in two;
He burns the chariots with fire.
Cease striving and know that I am God;
I will be exalted among the nations, I will be exalted in the earth.'
The LORD of hosts is with us;
The God of Jacob is our stronghold. ...

Today I am reminded of who He is to me. That He is always there, even in my Martha place, and nothing can separate me from His love. I am also gently shown how my constant 'striving' drives a slow but steady wedge between us.

The word 'strive' is defined in the Chambers English Dictionary as 'to try extremely hard; to struggle and to contend; to be in conflict'. Cambridge Dictionaries Online defines striving as 'to try very hard to do something or to make something happen, especially for a long time or against difficulties'. Both these definitions suggest hard work, a sense of constant pushing and straining. I know this feeling well; I have always felt that my life was a constant battle interspersed with brief periods of normality. Even as I have learned to walk with my Saviour, I have struggled to live in the truth of His words in Matthew 11:30: '*My yoke is easy and My burden is light.*'

Gently but firmly I am drawn again to focus on the words of the psalm above, written by the sons of Korah, and to meditate on the way they use images of nature to describe a relationship with God built on solid foundations. A relationship that is about stillness and faith in the midst of turmoil.

Therefore we will not fear, though the earth should change

How many times have sudden changes in my circumstances left me feeling as if the very earth underneath my feet has shifted uncontrollably? I have never been in a physical earthquake, but I imagine it must be one of the most terrifying experiences in the world. Where do you run to, when the very earth on which you stand trembles underneath your feet? How do you stand still when everything you have taken for granted is suddenly and swiftly taken away? How do you maintain your confidence in each day without constantly wondering if it is just a matter of time before everything comes crashing down again? I have seen many emotional earthquakes; the scars across the landscape of my heart are barely covered with newly grown confidence and inner strength. It feels sometimes as if the slightest tremor could reveal the trenches and fault lines.

I confess before Him that I have learned to live in fear of the earth changing beneath my feet. I work hard so I will have enough, I live in 'just-in-case mode' and I try, often unsuccessfully, to plan ahead for every eventuality. I strive to protect me and mine from the earthquakes, from the tremors, from the aftershocks. I feel myself growing incredibly weary sometimes with the effort of trying so hard, or being 'so responsible' for my own future and sometimes, for other people's. This place of striving, my Martha place, comes decorated with badly applied wallpaper of collapsed dreams, unfulfilled and silent promises, framed pictures of ravaged lands and uprooted hopes. Here, there is no memory of the rainbow that came after each storm, the new life that emerged from the ravaged soil; here I have learned to forget He who held my hand through the earthquake and calmed the storm within.

I think about the things that represent the stability of the earth beneath my feet to me – my home, my family, my health, my job, my finances, in no particular order. He shows me His hand over and in each of these things, and I know that in the face of His mercy and grace my strivings are like the single beat of a mosquito's wings in a dense rainforest. I hear Him ask:

> *And which of you by worrying can add a single hour to his life's span? If then you cannot do even a very little thing, why do you worry about other matters?*

> (Luke 12:25–26)

Yet I have done this for so long, Lord! He knows I want to let go, I want to feel the ropes I have held on to for so long slip through my fingers as I relinquish them to His firm hands. I want to sit down and rest my weary legs, I want to lift the weighty bag from my shoulders and stretch them out. I want to rest in His arms, curl up like a baby, place my head on His chest and hear the gentle rumble of His love soothe me to sleep like a babe. So I dwell on His words…

> *Come to Me, all who are weary and heavy-laden, and I will give you rest. Take My yoke upon you and learn from Me, for I am gentle and humble in heart, and YOU WILL FIND REST FOR YOUR SOULS*

> (Matthew 11:28–29)

He invites me into His rest. It is a special place… He is here and I can lay all these burdens at His feet. He admonishes me gently from the book of Isaiah 30:15–18, even as He did the Israelites, pointing out the futility and, indeed, the dangers of my own striving.

> *'In repentance and rest you will be saved,*
> *In quietness and trust is your strength.'*

But you were not willing,
And you said, 'No, for we will flee on horses,'
Therefore you shall flee!
'And we will ride on swift horses,'
Therefore those who pursue you shall be swift.
One thousand will flee at the threat of one man;
You will flee at the threat of five,
Until you are left as a flag on a mountain top
And as a signal on a hill.
Therefore the LORD longs to be gracious to you,
And therefore He waits on high to have compassion on you.
For the LORD is a God of justice;
How blessed are all those who long for Him.

He longs to be gracious to me, to invite me into a place of repentance, rest and salvation, of quietness and trust.

I sit quietly as I begin to understand that He alone is the solid ground underneath my feet. This mortal earth may indeed change, but He is the same as He has always been; He is the solid ground that never changes. My God of Abraham, my God of Isaac, Jacob, Joseph, Joshua… the same One who parted the Red Sea. I do not have to be afraid of this earth changing under my feet; I see that I need to stand firm in the knowledge that it will always change and that's OK because I do not stand on mortal ground. I stand on He who made the heavens and earth. Like a child I am carried on His shoulders, and as He stands astride the shifting earth, and commands it to be still, I know I am safe here.

And though the mountains slip into the heart of the sea …

(Psalm 46:2)

I picture mountains, indomitable, towering above everything else since the beginning of time. It is difficult to contemplate or imagine Mount Kilimanjaro or Everest slipping into the heart of the sea. Slippage suggests a slow but unstoppable process,

and I imagine nature railing against it, trying to hold on even as each mountain is subsumed by a sea that persistently gains ground, inch by inch, foot by foot, and swells with pride with each submerged victory.

This is no imagined fantasy; science confirms that the seas are full of submerged mountains. It is a process that cannot be stopped or held back, yet He tells me that for each part of creation disappearing beneath submerged victorious waves, another part of undiscovered territory is revealed somewhere, often unseen by human eyes but below His watchful gaze. The mountains are here to stay and both sea and mountains will be engaged in this waltz to the song of creation till the end of time. It is the way it is. Creation is His and nothing happens without His knowledge. He conducts this orchestra, He choreographs the waltz, He picked the dancers. They are but part of a bigger picture. Each submerged mountain becomes a gift home for teeming sea life, homes for millions of barnacles, fauna, anemones; no crook or cranny is wasted, there is purpose in all things.

I consider the 'slipping mountains' in my life… the things I am holding on to even as they slip away from me, as forces outside my control pull them away. Sometimes they are relationships; sometimes it's the things I think I desperately need to hold on to.

I recognise the fear I feel as these things feel as if they are slipping through my fingers. The fear that stems from a belief that without these things I am somehow not enough, I will not be enough. It is a fear based on a lack of understanding or realisation that He is more than enough for me.

I am drawn to Paul's inspirational statement in Philippians 4:11–13:

> Not that I speak from want, for I have learned to be content in whatever circumstances I am. I know how to get along with humble means, and I also know how to live in prosperity; in any and every circumstance I have learned the secret of being filled and going hungry, both of having abundance and suffering need. I can do all things through Him who strengthens me. (emphasis mine)

As I read these words afresh, I understand that my challenge is not to keep trying to stop things slipping through my fingers but rather to learn to open my hands and let them go so I can hold on to the one thing that matters – Him. I look down on my hands and it becomes clear that if they are holding on to Him, if I can just grasp the magnitude of Who and What He is, then nothing else *will* matter. Like the woman with the issue of blood in the Bible (see Luke 8:43–48), all I need to do is touch and hold the fringe of His gown. If I do, my hands, my heart, will be forever healed and full. These mountains may indeed slip into the sea but as with nature He is in control and if I trust in Him then He will continue to create new territory in my life even as He does in nature.

Cease striving, my child...

He tells me He wants more for me than this constant striving. He tells me I was made for so much more than this. His words bear no condemnation for my fevered effort, but rather sadness that I have not yet learned to trust Him enough. He knows I am weary, He knows how much I want to trust Him, to believe that He really is enough. He has compassion on me; He knows I am but dust. Yet He loves me still.

> *Just as a father has compassion on his children,*
> *So the LORD has compassion on those who fear Him.*
> *For He Himself knows our frame;*
> *He is mindful that we are but dust.*

> (Psalm 103:13–14)

His love is all-forgiving, all-encompassing. It is a father's arms around a wounded child, it is a mother's kiss on a fevered brow... it is the gentle breeze that dances across my skin, it is the sound of 1,000 angelic voices encompassed in a single whisper of His name, the only name – Jesus.

I am burdened, so I unpack my burdens. He shows me a backpack full of stones, each one marked with the name of a particular burden I carry. I have an inventory, and as I work my way down the list, I take it out and lay it at my Saviour's scarred feet.

> *My changing earth*
> *My disappearing mountains,*
> *My roaring, foaming waters,*
> *My fear, my worries, my sorrow.*
> *The list goes on...*

It feels so good to do this again, to know that I am not condemned. I imagine He raises His eyebrows gently as I take some of them out of my heavy backpack –'You still have that one in there? I thought we dealt with that one?' – He takes it nonetheless, and sets them all at the foot of the cross, where they seem to melt way. He breaks the arrows, the spears, He burns the chariots that have chased me. My bag is empty, I hold nothing back; I lay it all down. I feel light, released, free. I let go.

Mary's choice

Now He shows me Mary's choice. She chose the 'good part'. Jesus tells me that only 'God is good': *And Jesus said to him, "Why do you call Me good? No one is good except God alone"* (Mark 10:18).

Mary knew her Saviour. She saw Him as He was, and she sat at His feet. She knew that nothing could take that away from her, and Paul knew it too. In Romans 8:35–39, he captures it all when he says:

> *Who will separate us from the love of Christ? Will tribulation, or distress, or persecution, or famine, or nakedness, or peril, or sword? Just as it is written, 'FOR YOUR SAKE WE ARE BEING PUT TO DEATH ALL DAY LONG; WE WERE CONSIDERED AS SHEEP TO BE SLAUGHTERED.' But in all these things we overwhelmingly conquer through Him who loved us. For I am convinced that neither death, nor life, nor angels, nor principalities, nor things present, nor things to come, nor powers, nor height, nor depth, nor any other created thing, will be able to separate us from the love of God, which is in Christ Jesus our Lord.*

Martha worried, she struggled, contended and strived. Mary chose to sit at her Saviour's feet and listen. She focused on the one thing that she needed. The one thing that would never be moved or taken away. She would not and could not be moved, because the Lord delighted in her as she drank in His words and learned heavenly truths. She chose to be still, and in her stillness she learned the secret of contentment.

Evening truths

It is evening and the day is ending. I have learned, I have laid down. I have repented. I have been loved, restored, refreshed. I am at peace. I lay it all down. I sit at His feet. I drink in the stillness of His presence. I consider that He is the great I AM. He is my beginning and my end. He is my today and my tomorrow. All that I am, all that I ever will be, is in the palm of His hands. I am but a vapor, yet He loves me deeply, completely and thoroughly. Everything that is, is because He is. I consider, I ponder upon His words. My heart is stilled within me… I 'cease to strive', I am still and I know that He is God. He is God.

Note

I found the process of listing all my burdens really helpful. I didn't dwell on a specific issue or discuss each one. I did not feel this was what I was being asked to do on this day. I was just led to list them, so I wrote down everything I was worried about. It might be helpful to think of what they are in relation to this psalm (mountains, seas, changing earth) and recognise where you are striving. What is it you need to stop doing, and be still instead? I repented of my striving. I realised I was being disobedient. I asked for more trust and more faith, and then I sat and was still before Him.

My prayer

Dear Jesus,

I confess that I strive, that I worry all the time. I have brought this before You so many times and still I struggle to trust, to believe, to be still before You. Lord, I don't know why You love me so much, I don't understand the grace that means that You can forgive me every time, but I am so grateful for it. Help me, Lord, to be still before You; help me to know that You are the one thing, the only thing that matters. Lord Jesus, when the mountains crumble, when the earth shifts beneath my feet, when the winds blow and the clouds gather, help me to know You are right here by my side, always right here with me, and help me to be still under the safety of Your wings and know that You alone are God. Thank You, Jesus.

DAY 2 — Seated in Heavenly Places

ODAY MY VERSE comes from the book of Ephesians:

But God, being rich in mercy, because of His great love with which
He loved us, even when we were dead in our transgressions, made
us alive together with Christ (by grace you have been saved), and
raised us up with Him, and seated us with Him in the heavenly
places in Christ Jesus, so that in the ages to come He might show the
surpassing riches of His grace in kindness toward us in Christ Jesus.

(Ephesians 2:4–7)

I know this verse well. Today, however, I am challenged to understand exactly what it means to be seated with Jesus in the heavenly places. I am told it means I am a 'kingdom citizen'. I am not of this earth, even though I am physically here at the moment. I have been raised up with Christ, and in this heavenly place I have the opportunity to live life to a different frequency, to a new rhythm. A place where His will is done on earth as it is in heaven.

I am challenged to consider what this means for my daily walk with Him… to live physically on earth while spiritually operating from the heavenly places. Surely this calls for a different approach to life, a different perspective with which I view my daily existence, the highs and the lows. I am seated in heavenly places with the Saviour of the earth. In many ways this is too enormous to comprehend, understand, or even (dare I confess) believe.

I imagine having my own personal room in the White House or 10 Downing Street – a place I could come and go to whenever I needed, where I was important, loved, valued, and had access to limitless resources to meet my daily needs. How would that affect the way I lived, how I addressed challenges and issues? Would I retreat so quickly into my Martha place if I knew and really believed all that was available to me in the heavenly places?

Silently I wonder why I often find myself feeling like a prodigal child, living among the pigs, feeding from the slops when my Father has a rich mansion and a room prepared and waiting in which my every need is to be met with loving hands.

Many dwelling places…

In My Father's house are many dwelling places; if it were not so, I would have told you; for I go to prepare a place for you. If I go and prepare a place for you, I will come again and receive you to Myself, that where I am, there you may be also. (John 14:2–3)

Like many others, I had always imagined this verse referring to a place for my spirit when my physical body dies. Indeed, Jesus says it to His disciples at a time when He is preparing and comforting them in anticipation of His death and departure.

Yet today, the Holy Spirit challenges me to see this verse differently. In salvation, granted so freely to me when I believed in Him and confessed Him as my Saviour, I have already been raised up with Him, and by grace I am now seated alongside Him. I am 'where He is'. This is not just a promise based on a future post-death experience, it is a 'now' reality here on earth. When I walk with Him, when I abide in His presence, I move into this space that He has prepared for me. I walk each day in the glory of His presence and by His side. I am a natural being living in a supernatural reality.

The realisation that He has prepared a special place for me, which is available to me right now, is overwhelming, followed swiftly by a conviction and sadness as I see that I am spending too much time away from this place. I know that my own self-doubt, a wrong belief in my own insignificance, keeps me waiting at the door, peering in through the window, not quite believing that this place which has been purchased with the blood of a gracious Saviour, is mine. It feels like I am spending time living in my old car outside a beautiful mansion with my name on the deeds. I am a lottery winner with the winning ticket crumpled in my purse while I beg and borrow to survive each day.

Yet, oh, what joy, what creativity, what abundance awaits me inside. The Lord reminds me of the parable told by my Saviour about a host at a banquet awaiting his guests:

A certain man was preparing a great banquet and invited many guests. At the time of the banquet he sent his servant to tell those who had been invited, 'Come, for everything is now ready.' But they all alike began to make excuses. The first said, 'I have just bought a field, and I must go and see it. Please excuse me.' Another said, 'I have just bought five yoke of oxen, and I'm on my way to try them out. Please excuse me.' Still another said, 'I have just got married, so I can't come.' The servant came back and reported this to his master. Then the

*owner of the house became angry and ordered his servant,
'Go out quickly into the streets and alleys of the town and
bring in the poor, the crippled, the blind and the lame.' 'Sir,'
the servant said, 'what you ordered has been done, but there
is still room.' Then the master told his servant, 'Go out to the
roads and country lanes and compel them to come in, so that
my house will be full. I tell you, not one of those who were
invited will get a taste of my banquet.'*

(Luke 14:16–24, NIV UK 2011)

My prayer

Dear Jesus,

I am so sorry that I keep You waiting time and time again,
like a very rude guest. I want to be in this place with You,
Lord, this place You have prepared for me. It is true that
I don't feel worthy to be there, but I am learning that this
is OK. You have not asked me to come in fine clothes, You
have asked me to come as I am, and I am so grateful for that.
Thank You that in You there is room for me and that here, in
Your place, Lord, I fit perfectly, even if I don't fit anywhere
else. Thank You, Jesus.

In faith, I step into these heavenly places… this house of
many rooms… and the Holy Spirit takes my hand and leads
me through. I am given a full tour of many rooms…

Heavenly places: Victory's place

Thy will be done in earth, as it is in heaven.

(Matthew 6:10, KJV)

In this heavenly place in which I sit alongside my beloved Saviour,
all is according to the will of my heavenly Father. In His will and
through His grace He has raised up Jesus and given Him authority
over all things.

These are in accordance with the working of the strength of His might which He brought about in Christ, when He raised Him from the dead and seated Him at His right hand in the heavenly places, far above all rule and authority and power and dominion, and every name that is named, not only in this age but also in the one to come. And He put all things in subjection under His feet, and gave Him as head over all things to the church, which is His body, the fullness of Him who fills all in all.

(Ephesians 1:19–23)

He is above every rule, power, dominion and authority that exists here on earth. I am reminded that here on earth in my physical body, I live in a place where the one that Jesus describes as the *'ruler of this world'* has dominion. (John 12:31) In this 'world' of evil, confusion, sickness, death, greed, poverty, lack, strife, death and destruction reign, yet I abide with my heavenly Father in a place where the Son, my Saviour, reigns supreme over all these things, and because He does, I do too. In this place I have victory over everything that sends me fleeing to my Martha place in fear and defeat.

I have told you these things, so that in me you may have peace. In this world you will have trouble. But take heart! I have overcome the world.

(John 16:33, NIV UK 2011)

In this 'room', this heavenly place of victory, I see a young David pick up five stones and I am taught to find similar stones by the river of God's Word. I am taught to equip my sling, and to hold my arm poised to release my spiritual stones right into the eye of the giant enemy. I am taught to bear the sword of the truth of God's Word over me and cut off the head of the lying giant. I repeat after David:

Blessed be the LORD, my rock,
Who trains my hands for war,

And my fingers for battle;
My lovingkindness and my fortress,
My stronghold and my deliverer ...

(Psalm 144:1–2)

This victorious place feels so much better than my Martha place. Here I feel powerful, lifted, loved, protected. This is a place of victorious living, a place where He reigns over all that concerns me. I want to learn to live here victoriously and abundantly in Him. I am taught that this means living each day in the expectancy that all will be as He wills it, knowing that His will for me is always perfect. Here, I do not have to live in fear of the enemy having success in my life, or in deference to his authority through sickness, lack, fear, doubt or even persecution, challenges or difficulties. There will be troubles, but He has overcome and through Him, so have I. Not even death can separate me from His love; there is no problem bigger that Him, no giant that cannot be slain in the power of His love and Word.

My prayer

Dear Holy Spirit of the Living God,
Oh, Teacher, Counsellor and Friend, I confess I do not know how to stay in the place of victory; it is too easy for me to revert into my Martha place, a place of defeat and despair, but I want to live in Him. I want to live victoriously and abundantly in Him! So I submit myself to You and ask that You teach me, lead me and show me the way. I ask in His name, that His name may be glorified in me and that my heavenly Father's name may be glorified through Him. In Jesus' name. Amen.

Wisdom's place

This is Wisdom's place, too, a place where Wisdom cries out to me, offering me the opportunity to delve into mysteries beyond my understanding. A place where I am offered an alternative to the false safety I find in my Martha place.

Trust in the LORD with all your heart
And do not lean on your own understanding.

(Proverbs 3:5)

Here I am overwhelmed with the gifts on offer: understanding, wholesome advice, good judgement, discernment, insight and strength (see Proverbs 8). These gifts, carved in shapes that make it impossible to fit them into my Martha place, merge together here in perfect symmetry, flowing in fluid formation around me as I walk through them, filling my heart and head with emotions and feelings too dazzling to explain.

I am unable to fit them in my arms, and with each handful, each gift multiplies and I understand that I could never take all that I am being offered; there is more than I can ask for, more than I will ever need.

In this place of understanding I see the extent of the love of Him who made the stars and put them in their place, of He who carved the universe and set each planet in the sky. Covered with discernment, the words of Scripture take on a new life and leap out of the pages at me, becoming living answers to my prayers. Here in delight I am taught to recognise the voice of the Holy Spirit within me, to sit at His feet as He teaches me, to be still as He calls me to account as I begin to strive...

Now we have received, not the spirit of the world, but the Spirit who is from God, so that we may know the things freely given to us by God, which things we also speak, not in words taught by human wisdom, but in those taught by the Spirit, combining spiritual thoughts with spiritual words.

(1 Corinthians 2:12–13)

My mouth opens and I speak a language that I do not know. Arm in arm with Wisdom, I sing praises to a God who is beyond all understanding, yet humbled Himself that I may know and understand, even if just in part. My eyes are opened to the locks in my Martha place; I unlock the doors and break down the walls, armed with the strength that comes from knowledge of who I am in Him.

I look in His eyes and feel the walls of my Martha place begin to come tumbling down. I am filled with His Wisdom... I am overwhelmed with His truth, and in His truth I am free...

> *So Jesus was saying to those Jews who had believed Him, 'If you continue in My word, then you are truly disciples of Mine; and you will know the truth, and the truth will make you free.'*
>
> (John 8:32)

My Wisdom place prayer

Lord, I thank You that You have sent Wisdom to call out to me as I walk by, that You have given her so many gifts to give me and that through her and in her I learn of Your love for me, Your plans for me, and the beauty of Your thoughts towards me. I thank You that though she is invaluable, more precious than the purest gold or silver, that I can have her freely because You love me and have freely provided her to me through the Holy Spirit and in the blood of Christ Jesus. Lord, forgive me for searching for wisdom in the wrong places, and teach me to find her, to listen to her and to spend time in her presence, in Your presence, that I may grow in stature and in wisdom before You. I ask in Jesus' name. Amen.

A place of repentance, reconciliation and forgiveness

I come to the place of the cross. A room where my sins are laid out and bare, and as I seek to turn away in shame and guilt before the wounded Lamb of God, I am held in my Father's embrace.

> *[If] My people who are called by My name humble themselves and pray and seek My face and turn from their wicked ways, then I will hear from heaven, will forgive their sin and will heal*

their land. Now My eyes will be open and My ears attentive to the prayer offered in this place. For now I have chosen and consecrated this house that My name may be there forever, and My eyes and My heart will be there perpetually.

(2 Chronicles 7:14–16)

It is dark, but in my hands I am holding a light. His light, and I am guided to the cross. In this heavenly place, where I am reminded of the price He paid on the cross to redeem me, the light I hold glows brighter and brighter till the room is illuminated totally by His love for me.

There is no condemnation here, just love. I have nothing to offer except my true repentance, yet it seems that in this place that is enough, and as I speak His name, I am offered beauty for my ashes, new robes to replace my old and stained shirt, I am given bags of joy, reams of hope. Once again, a Father who cannot seem to stop heaping good gifts on me overwhelms me. My heart is full of gifts that I do not deserve, yet I seem to keep getting.

My place of forgiveness
prayer

Thank You, Lord Jesus, that you died on the cross for me so that I could have forgiveness in You. Thank You that You have taken my burdens, my guilt, my shame, my broken pieces, and You have made them whole by the power of Your love for me. Thank You for Your love that overwhelms me in this place; thank You, Lord Jesus. I love You so very much!

The throne room

Therefore let us draw near with confidence to the throne of grace, so that we may receive mercy and find grace to help in time of need.

(Hebrews 4:16)

How do I describe the throne room of the King of kings, or the place where all that is, is as it was, is and will be now and forever? I am allowed in here, in this place of majesty beyond all description, in this place where the cherubim and seraphim's cries of glory fill the air, where the chosen ones sit in splendid purity, here where the son Himself sits at the right hand of God. Here, where light shines brighter than light itself, where the presence of the God of all creation manifestly defies all laws of space, time, present, past and future... I am welcome here! I am allowed to walk up to the throne and ask for mercy and grace, for healing and provision. I am made worthy by the robes I wear, given to me by the Prince of Peace Himself. I walk past the temple gates, I walk past creatures I cannot describe, past the hosts of angels crying 'Hosanna', past the beautiful ones of God, till I am standing before the throne of grace, mercy and peace. I do not need to ask, I do not need to plead my case. Here He knows, I am known, and all is as He made it to be. I stand, and in this place, all I can be is still. Like the cherubim in Exodus 25:20 I am taught that my face and my eyes must be turned constantly to Him who sits on the mercy seat, above the law, above all else. Here I can listen, here I can hear.

> *There I will meet with you; and from above the mercy seat, from between the two cherubim which are upon the ark of the testimony, I will speak to you about all that I will give you in commandment for the sons of Israel.*

(Exodus 25:22)

My throne room prayer

Lord, You know that I am not confident in approaching the throne of grace. You know that too often I allow my inner critic, the voices of condemnation and the lies of the enemy to convince me that I am not worthy to enter this place. Yet, Lord, as I stand here and survey that which my limited mind can comprehend, I realise that the truth is, I could never be worthy enough to enter Your throne room. I have the right of entry here not because of who I am or ever could be, but because of who You are and because Jesus, Your son, who died for me and for my sins, sits at Your right hand and bids me come to Him. Holy Spirit, please teach me to approach the throne of grace and to find mercy and grace in my time of need. In Jesus' name. Amen.

An abundant place – the treasury place

Do not store up for yourselves treasures on earth, where moth and rust destroy, and where thieves break in and steal. But store up for yourselves treasures in heaven, where neither moth nor rust destroys, and where thieves do not break in or steal; for where your treasure is, there your heart will be also.

(Matthew 6:19–21)

I am allowed to peek inside this room, and I marvel at the rows of shelves and storage spaces. This is my storage space, and on each shelf the labels tell me the indexing system – acts of kindness, acts of grace, compassion, mercy, faith, joy, love, forgiveness, peacekeeping, Word-spreading. The sheer variety of opportunities to populate this place with treasures of heaven amazes me, and I am driven by an urgency to fill this place while I still have breath within me. This is my eternal pension; my savings investments for all eternity. There is no financial advisor here, no investment rules and regulations. Just His Word written in blazing letters that simply says:

Love as I have loved you

I realise I can no longer spend time in my Martha place worrying about material goods and human treasures that seem to grow old even while brand new. Here there are so many empty shelves and spaces to fill with works He has set out for me. Here there is no space for gorgeous houses, cars, clothes and other material necessities… in this place they crumble as dust.

Arms laden with heavenly gifts, senses overwhelmed with the abundance of heaven itself, I want to give back more, so much more; I want to do more, be more than a woman trapped by the chains of her past and lost in the muddles of her present. I think of all the wasted moments and times and I lift my eyes, resolute to focus on the One who gave His all for me. I step away from the door…

My treasure room prayer

Heavenly Father, maker of heaven and earth and all that dwells therein,

I thank You that You have given me access to build my treasures in heaven through generosity and grace towards those in need. Teach me to walk in this, Lord; Holy Spirit, please convict me when I begin to focus more on earthly riches than on my treasures in heaven. Lord, let my heart dwell in this place, because if my heart is here, then I will be too. Thank You, Lord, for Your generosity, favour and provision towards me, and Lord, I promise to use everything that You give me for Your glory in whatever way I can. In Jesus' name I pray. Amen.

Seated in heavenly places

My tour is ended, yet I realise there is still so much that I have not seen and will not see while I still breathe the air of this earth. This is my Father's house, and here my Lord Jesus has prepared a place for me. He has worked so hard to make it just right. His sweat and tears fell to the ground as He laboured and built, His blood ran red with the effort, His hands and feet were torn, His side ripped, and it was only as He gave it all that He announced that it was finished, it was ready for me. It was done! How can I spend time seated in Martha places, places of regret, sorrow, lack, want, despair, when there are so many rooms prepared here for me at so great a price?

As I wake each morning, I know now I can consciously make a choice about the heavenly places I will spend time in each day. As I rise, my spirit takes its seat according to my faith, my hope, my heart, and His power at work within me. I look back at my Martha place, the door is still open... inside I can see the shadows of the person I had become, the buckets of tears unshed and overflowing, the unpacked boxes of my past, the unfinished hand-drawn plans and maps to my future. I see the broken furniture, the empty plates, and I am ashamed that I have allowed myself to dwell in such spiritual squalor when I was made for so much more. I am convicted by the quiet grace of my Saviour, and the forgiveness in His embrace. Yet even as I turn away, I hear the mocking, whispering voices from the shadows: 'You will be back. You like it here. You can't stay away. You will be back.'

Perhaps they are right in part. Perhaps if this was just my choice, if I had to stay away in my own power, I would indeed find my way back. Like an addict unable to resist, I would return, but I have learned one thing about the heavenly places among all things. Here He has the authority, and in this place I am shielded, made whole, filled with supernatural power. I will close this door not because I am strong, but because He is strong in me. It may take time to push it shut, to silence the voices, to walk away and never to look back, but I know I will do it. My steps will falter, but then I will find my way to the mercy seat and kneel in forgiveness and receive His love and grace. I know my way there now. I can do all things through Him who gives me strength, and I am free in Him.

I turn to Wisdom's place and see her smile at me through my tears; I feel my sling in my pocket and roll my fingers around the smooth stones of His words. His sword of truth weighs lightly on my waist, and my hands overflow with His generosity and gifts. Here is life, and these are my heavenly places...

My prayer

Dear Jesus,
I am so sorry that I have spent so much time worrying about the unimportant things. I am so sorry that I have spent so much time focusing on the earthly places when You gave so

much to secure a seat for me by Your side. I know it will take me time to get this one right – to understand how to walk each day in heavenly places, but I thank You that You sent the Holy Spirit to teach me and to lead me to You.

Holy Spirit, I open my mind and heart to You now; please teach me. I know He is the way, the truth and the life, and I want to sit with Him in glory and live according to the will and purposes of my heavenly Father. Holy Spirit, please teach me to spend each day in these heavenly places, to operate my earthly life from these places and to do all I can to return here for ever when my work is done on earth. I promise to incline my ears and my heart towards You as You teach and to do all I can to walk in obedience. When I sin and fall, and I know I will, I promise to make my way to the throne room, knowing that I will find forgiveness, mercy and grace.

I repent of my ignorance and sins, and I thank You, Father, for my Saviour, and all that has been done for me. In Jesus' name. Amen.

Notes

This was the most vivid and startling of all the lessons I learnt during my 7 days, and my spiritual 'tour' around the rooms felt like a vision and a dream combined into one. As I got to the end of the day and began to write it down what had become clearer to me was the very many different facets of the relationship that we are each privileged to share with God the Father, Jesus Christ and the Holy Spirit and how full, abundant and rich it is. I began to understand that in the presence of such riches, depth and love I had more than I would ever need and want. I am in awe of the fact that we have access to all of this because He loves us. Spend time in each room in your own way, tarry a while and hear Him whisper to you. These are your places too and in them there is peace and love beyond measure.

You ask and do not receive, because you ask with wrong motives, so that you may spend it on your pleasures.

(James 4:3)

TODAY I AM CHALLENGED by my heavenly Father about my 'asking habits'. Like a child caught with a hand in a biscuit jar, I flush with guilt when the Lord gently raises this in my spirit. It is an issue I have struggled with and one that often sits poorly hidden in layers of confusion, guilt and hurt and mostly disappointment that has silently evolved into hidden doubt and disbelief.

> *Ask, and it will be given to you; seek, and you will find; knock, and it will be opened to you. For everyone who asks receives, and he who seeks finds, and to him who knocks it will be opened.*

(Matthew 7:7)

Do I really believe these words with all my heart, or rather do I just believe they do not apply to me? As always, He knows and He sees. Nothing is hidden from Him. He knows that each time I have seen my prayers go unanswered I have allowed a little brittle chip of disappointment, doubt and unbelief to settle deep in the recesses of my heart. He has seen the growing pile of chips and watched as they have begun to form a wall of hardness between us. He knows I have ceased praying for certain things, convinced that His silence stems either from my unworthiness or because He cannot hear me. My faith is a thin veneer for my disbelief and doubt, my unspoken questions a silent shadow over my relationship with a Father who I know loves me beyond my comprehension.

He does not condemn me, but He asks me if I think there could be a better way; am I asking the right way?

> *You ask and do not receive, because you ask with wrong motives, so that you may spend it on your pleasures.*

(James 4:3)

I admit truthfully that when I read James' blunt scripture above, an inner defensiveness and resentment rises up within me. 'That's a bit harsh,' I say silently. 'I don't agree that I have always asked with "wrong motives". It has not always been about wanting to spend things on my own pleasures.

'Besides,' I continue as I reason with my heavenly Father (who is wisdom personified), 'what about all the other people who ask for things and don't receive them – prayers for healing for loved ones that never comes, poverty, desperation… surely these are not just about pleasure? Is it not too easy to just say they have asked the wrong way? Surely some of those people deserved to have their prayers answered?' I lift my eyes to my Father and say plaintively, 'I don't understand.'

'No,' He says gently. 'You don't understand.'

Learning to ask…

I am overflowing with questions: 'How should I ask? What should I say? Is there a right way and a wrong way? Are there things it's OK to ask for and things that are not? When is my asking selfish in its design? If I ask for things that are just about me? Is that wrong and selfish in a world where so many hunger and thirst? My Lord Jesus says that my heavenly Father "knows I have need of these things" – do I really believe that He knows all the things I need? And how does He sort my needs from my wants? I have so many questions!'

I know I worry about things all the time; it is the thing I spend most of my time doing in my Martha place. Most of my worries are linked to things I believe I want, need or lack. These are not always material things; sometimes it's about emotions, peace, a desire to be more, to be less, to just be. Sometimes it's about other people, my job, my family… the list is endless. Yet even as I explore this endless list, I am brought to the realisation of what a 'fleshy' list it is. These things I worry most about, the things that form the reservoir from which my desperate requests are drawn, are indeed things of 'the flesh', 'things of this world', and in Romans 8:5–6 Paul says:

> For those who are according to the flesh set their minds on the things of the flesh, but those who are according to the spirit, the things of the Spirit. For the mind set on the flesh is death, but the mind set on the Spirit is life and peace …

There is a light bulb beginning to flicker in my brain as I understand that if my mind is weighted and dead, it is hardly likely to communicate effectively with the source of all life itself – God! It is no surprise that the next verse reads:

> *because the mind set on the flesh is hostile toward God; for it does not subject itself to the law of God, for it is not even able to do so … (v. 7)*

The words '*for it is not even able to do so*' cuts into my soul and I begin to understand why my mind seems to have an errant life of its own when I am in my Martha place. Often overwhelmed by my worries, I know I should pray, yet this is the very time when the words seem to dry out before they even reach my lips. Driven by shame, guilt, disbelief, I bury myself in other quick sources of empty comfort… inane TV shows, food, mindless conversations, or just tears.

These are the times when the scriptural promises of asking and receiving seem at their most empty in my mind, and when doubt and disbelief comes creeping in with long, cloying and winding tentacles. I know the Scriptures, I sing the songs, so why do I find myself here again and again?

'Oh, Lord,' I cry in despair. 'What hope is there for me?' I recall Paul's similar cry in Romans 7:15:

> *I do not understand what I do. For what I want to do I do not do, but what I hate I do.*

(NIV UK 2011)

I want to believe. I don't want to be in this place anymore. I want to surrender into His arms and know that all will be OK, and that even if the answers don't come when I need them, I will stay strong knowing I can trust in His will for me always. This is how I want to live… this is what I want to be!

As I bow before Him in despair, He gently draws my attention to my Saviour's prayer to His heavenly Father in John chapter 17

– the High Priest's prayer. I have read it before so it is not new, but this time I am encouraged to spend time with the text, to dive deep into the nuances, the words, the intimacy of the dialogue. I am encouraged to learn from it, and willingly I do. I close my eyes, still my heart before Him, listen and learn...

A High Priest's prayer – John 17

It is the night when Judas betrays Jesus and He is brought before the Jewish priests. Jesus is trying to prepare His disciples for the hard times ahead. Starting in John 14, He comforts His disciples, telling them:

> *Do not let your heart be troubled; believe in God, believe in Me.* (v. 1)

In John 15, Jesus tells them about the vine and the branches, He urges them to love one another, and in John 16, He promises them the Holy Spirit. By John 17, He has told them all He has to say at that time and He turns His attention upwards, towards His heavenly Father. The prayer that has been called the High Priest's prayer is beautiful, from a faithful and obedient Son to a Father that He has total and complete trust in. There is no doubt here, no questioning, no uncertainty... They are One, and in this prayer He asks that I too am made one with them, that we all are.

His words are a lesson in communication with our heavenly Father. In this prayer He makes several major requests of His Father, and my attention is drawn to His way. In Matthew 6:9–13 Jesus teaches us the Lord's Prayer. It is a direct response to the disciples' request. In John 17, however, there is no direct attempt to teach the disciples to pray, yet the fact that it is so carefully recorded word by word by John's faithful hands is no coincidence. There are lessons to be learned, seeds to be nurtured. I read and I learn.

Lifting my eyes to the hills...

Jesus spoke these things; and lifting up His eyes to heaven, He said ...

(John 17:1)

It is not the first time we read these words in the Bible. Just before Jesus calls Lazarus forth from the dead in John 11:1–44, John records that He 'raised His eyes' (v. 41) before beginning to speak to His Father.

On both these occasions, Jesus is surrounded by anxious and worried people... grieving at the death of Lazarus, and then the disciples trying to understand His warning of a dark and ominous few days ahead for all of them. There is no doubting His love and compassion for the suffering of those around Him, yet on both occasions He lifts His attention and gaze away from everything around Him to focus on the source of His strength and help. I imagine Him standing and raising His eyes to the heavens, His gentle eyes fixed on high.

I think of my bowed head when I pray... my closed eyes, and the reality of a brain that often develops a life of its own as I try to focus on my prayers. It is even worse when I am in my Martha place. It's hard to lift my eyes when I am so worried about the pots, pans, baggage and bags of life, or when my eyes are so focused on my problems.

In Psalm 121, the psalmist says:

> *I lift up my eyes to the mountains – where does my help come from? My help comes from the LORD, the Maker of heaven and earth.*

> (Psalm 121:1–2)

If my help comes from up above, then surely I must raise my eyes to Him, even as Jesus does. This is more than a physical act of gazing towards the sky or my ceiling, but an actual lifting of the eyes of my heart towards Him and away from the things of the world. It's choosing to focus my attention away from the natural and to gaze intently into His supernatural presence.

I am reminded of the old hymn…

> *Turn your eyes upon Jesus,*
> *Look full in His wonderful face,*
> *And the things of earth will grow*
> *strangely dim,*
> *In the light of His glory and grace.*

> (Helen Howarth Lemmel, 1863–1961)

It becomes clear to me then, as I lift my eyes to Him, as I engage fully with His countenance, that this impacts directly on the very things I pray for. There is a peace that comes from turning my eyes up to Him… an assurance that is captured in the rest of Psalm 121:

> *He will not let you stumble; the one who watches over you will not slumber.*
> *Indeed, he who watches over Israel never slumbers or sleeps.*
> *The LORD himself watches over you! The LORD stands beside you as your protective shade.*
> *The sun will not harm you by day, nor the moon at night.*

The Lord keeps you from all harm and watches over your life.
The Lord keeps watch over you as you come and go, both
now and forever.

(Psalm 121:3–8, NLT)

He watches over me from above, He is my Father 'which art in
heaven' (Matthew 6:9, KJV), and I am learning to lift my eyes to the
heavens...

For my Father's glory

Father, the hour has come; glorify Your Son, that the Son may
glorify You ...

(John 17:1)

It is not surprising that having connected with His Father, everything
that Jesus asks for is within the context of bringing glory to His
Father's name. Everything that Jesus does and asks for is about the
Father.

Yet rarely do I ask for things purely within the context of
bringing glory to my heavenly Father. How often do I connect
my needs and wants with the impact these things would have
on my ministry, my purpose for Him? If I am here to do His
will and bring glory to Him, then surely everything that I ask of
Him should be about fulfilling that purpose in some shape or
form – a bigger house, for instance, becomes a place in which
I can hold more events for fellow Christians, help more people
in need, share with the less fortunate, that His name may be
glorified through me. The purpose of all my blessings should be
to bless others.

I wonder silently and perhaps selfishly to myself if this approach
would limit the things I can ask Him for. In response I hear the Holy
Spirit ask me if there is anything I could want or have that I could not
use in some way, to glorify His name? If I am walking in His will, then
everything I want or need reflects who I am or want to be in Him.

The Spirit shows me the potential of living a life where everything that I own, have and want is tuned into the purpose of helping me to be fruitful and bringing glory to my Father, and how easy it is to ask my heavenly Father for things when they are part of this agenda. I am drawn to the words of the Lord Jesus in John 15:7–8:

> But if you remain in me and my words remain in you, you may ask for anything you want, and it will be granted! When you produce much fruit, you are my true disciples. This brings great glory to my Father.

(NLT)

I want to bring glory to Him... I love my heavenly Father and I want Him to be proud of me. I learn that instead of limiting my requests, this actually broadens the horizons of my engagement with Him. It provides a space in which I can work with Him and my Saviour, Jesus. We can co-produce, see His will done on earth as it is in heaven.

I begin to understand James' statement more, and I see the link between my asking and my giving. Giving to others and giving glory to my Father in all things.

My prayer

Dear Father,

I am so grateful for Your promise that You will perfect all that concerns me. Father, I want to live my life to bring glory to Your name. I want everything that I do and everything that I have, want and need to be connected to my core purpose to glorify Your kingdom. Father, I lay down my selfish desires before the throne of grace and ask that You fill me with a yearning for Your kingdom. Help me to recognise what I need for this journey, Lord, and what I can leave behind. Help me to trust in Your provision for me. Open my eyes and help me to understand how I can use Your blessings to be a blessing to others, and help me trust in the fact that You know what I need and You will add all those things to me according to Your will and for Your glory. Father, let Your name be glorified through me, through my deeds and my actions. In Jesus' name. Amen.

From a place of obedience

Jesus prays in a place of total obedience to His Father, even though He has not yet faced the cross:

> *I glorified You on the earth, having accomplished the work which You have given me to do.*

(John 17:4)

I understand that we are not saved by works, but it stands to reason that when making requests of my heavenly Father I need to be standing in a place of obedience to His will for and in my life. It is sometimes uncomfortable for us to remember the emphasis that Jesus places on living in obedience to His commandments. John 14:15: 'If you love me, you will obey my commandments' (GNT). Jesus lived and walked in complete obedience to His heavenly Father. Philippians 2:8–9 says:

> *Being found in appearance as a man, He humbled Himself by becoming obedient to the point of death, even death on a cross. For this reason also, God highly exalted Him, and bestowed on Him the name which is above every name ...*

I am reminded gently of all the times I have lifted my hands to the Lord even though I have been aware that I was not standing in a place of obedience to His will. I know He does not expect me to be perfect, He understands too well my human failings and weaknesses, but I also know that I have a responsibility to choose to abide in His will, where those weaknesses and failings are gently perfected and transformed through Him. I have a responsibility and ability to choose to be fruitful in all things as I abide in Him. Above all I can obey the greatest commandment He has given me – to love the Lord with all my heart, my soul and my mind, and to love my neighbour as myself.

Then I too can come before my Father and say: 'I have glorified You, Lord, by living my life as You have asked me to, and I am accomplishing the work You asked me to.'

In John 15:7 Jesus says to His disciples:

> *But if you remain in me and my words remain in you, you may ask for anything you want, and it will be granted!. When you produce much fruit you are my true disciples. This brings great glory to my Father...*

Obedience and fruitfulness are interlinked in the Kingdom and by His words and actions, Jesus teaches us the importance of asking from a place of both.

From a place of generosity

Jesus asks on behalf of the disciples. His request is devoid of self-interest: '*I ask on their behalf ...*' (John 17:9)

I know this does not preclude me from making requests about the things I need for me and mine, yet I am taught an important lesson here about 'generous asking'. I hated maths as a child, so when I am asked to imagine a prayer pie chart I am not amused. I realise rather shamefully that on many days mine would look like this –

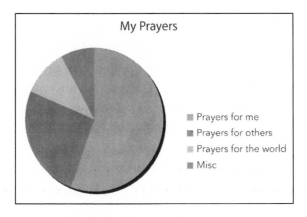

I am shown the importance of releasing the power that I have been given to benefit others. To love others as I love myself is not just about what I do in direct interaction with them, but also what I can do on their behalf. I think about the times when I have said 'I will pray for you' then forgotten to pray, or prayed just the once. I learn that generous prayer that reaches up on behalf of others must become part of my prayer life too.

When Jesus teaches His disciples the Lord's Prayer, it is interesting that He uses the word 'us' and not 'me'. Thus, even though He urges that the prayer should be done in private, the words demonstrate that the prayer should be made on behalf of others: 'Give *us* this day our daily bread' (Matthew 6:11, emphasis mine).

My prayer

Dear Holy Spirit,

Please teach me to pray on behalf of others around me. Let my prayers be filled more with requests for the needs of others than mine, because I know that the prayers of the righteous avail much (James 5:16) and that when we pray for others, we draw on an open heaven from which Your grace flows forth. I know that when I do this, You take care of my needs because You are a loving Father. Teach me to be a generous prayer. Amen.

From a place of God-given identity

Jesus asks from a place of complete knowledge and faith in who He is in His Father and their relationship – *even as You gave Him authority over all flesh, that to all whom You have given Him, He may give eternal life*' (John 17:2). So many times in this prayer, He reiterates the relationship He shares with His Father. It is intimate and incredibly powerful. I do not think He needs to say it to remind God or, indeed, purely for the benefit of the listeners. It is a celebration of their relationship, of their intimacy, and I learn that I want and need to celebrate the intimacy of my relationship with my Father when I come to Him. He has spoken words over me, directly and through others; I know who I am, I know what has been done for me, and I know that I am His.

My prayer

You are my Father, I am your beloved daughter; You gave Your only Son for me that I may have eternal life. Through Him I have life and in Him, by the power of His name, I have authority over the powers of darkness... in You, my Father, and in Jesus, my redeemer, I have eternal life. Thank You, Father.

I try repeating these words as I pray, and feel the strength and peace that flows over me as I state my relationship with My Father. 'I am my beloved's and [He] is mine' (Song of Solomon 6:3).

From a place of clarity

It is a long prayer, but it is clear and focused, bringing to mind Jesus' words when He teaches us the Lord's Prayer:

> And when you are praying, do not use meaningless repetitions as the Gentiles do, for they suppose that they will be heard for their many words. So do not be like them; for your Father knows what you need before you ask Him.
>
> (Matthew 6:7–8)

In this prayer in John 17, Jesus makes a clear distinction between what He is asking for and what He isn't: 'I do not ask *You to take them out of the world, but to keep them from the evil one*' (John 17:15, emphasis mine).

He also differentiates between what He 'wants' and what He 'desires'. It is a subtle but important difference: '*Father, I* desire *that they also, whom You have given Me, be with Me where I am, so that they may see My glory which You have given Me, for You loved Me before the foundation of the world'* (John 17:24, emphasis mine). His qualification of this request as a 'desire' reflects His recognition that this is His Father's decision, not His by right, despite the authority that has been given to Him. In Matthew 20:23, when asked by an anxious mother if her sons could sit at His right and left hand, He says: *'But to sit on My right or on My left, this is not Mine to give; but it is for those for whom it has been prepared'* (Mark 10:40).

I think about the things I 'desire', the things I want and the things I need, and I resolve to be clearer in my prayers with each one; to recognise those things I have no right to want but can express as a desire, trusting in my Father's judgement to make the best decision for me and for others. There is peace in that.

Eventide

This has been a long lesson to learn, and I am not sure I have learned it all yet. I understand now that to ask my Father is to have a dialogue with Him. It is to be specific, to stand in a place of obedience, clarity and trust. It is to turn my eyes towards Him, to step out of my Martha place and to ask with confidence and faith in the beauty of His eternal will.

I have learned that I need to know who I am in Him when I come to the throne of grace, and that it is this trust in who He is that resolves and melts away the brittleness. I read and see Jesus' complete trust and love for His Father, and I know I want to imitate Him in this. I want to believe the promises and stand on His Word, and I resolve to do so.

Does this mean I will see every prayer answered, every request granted? I know it doesn't, but then I also know that *'faith is the assurance of things hoped for, the conviction of things not seen'* (Hebrews 11:1), but true faith comes in placing the request before the throne and trusting that He is able to do so much more with my prayers and requests than I can ever imagine. All I need to do is to trust and believe in the perfection of His love for me, and ask that His will be done on earth as it is in heaven.

> *Now to Him who is able to do far more abundantly beyond all that we ask or think,* according to the power that works within us, *to Him be the glory in the church and in Christ Jesus to all generations forever and ever. Amen.*

> (Ephesians 3:20, emphasis mine)

I feel the brittleness begin to dissolve, and I see why this is important to my relationship with Him. This is our dialogue, this is our space. Ultimately, the requests themselves are insignificant; the power lies in the faith, trust and obedience that informs my asking, my visit to the throne room.

'I think I understand, Father. I am sorry for my disbelief.'

'I think you are beginning to,' He says.

'I love You, righteous Father.'

'I love you too, My beloved child.'

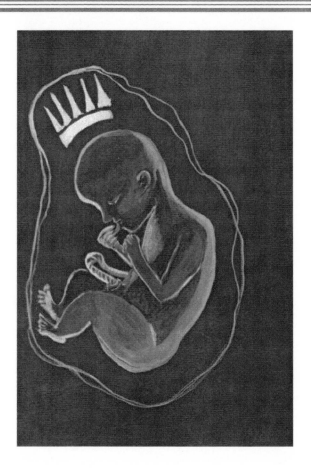

Are not two sparrows sold for a cent? And yet not one of them will fall to the ground apart from You Father. But the very hairs of your head are all numbered. So do not fear; you are more valuable than many sparrows.

(Matthew 10:29–31)

TODAY, ON THE fourth day, the Lord draws me to this passage. I try hard to understand what it means to have the very hairs on my head numbered by God. It is too much for me to comprehend. I think of the billions of Christians across the world, in every different continent, and the knowledge that He has numbered the hairs on each of our heads is totally incomprehensible to me. Far more so if I extend my thinking to those who are yet to believe, all of humanity. Yet it must be true, because Jesus speaks these words and there is no untruth in Him. He is the Word of God breathed into flesh for the redemption of humankind.

In my Martha place I forget how intentional God's love is for me. It is so easy to sink into a place where my life seems to be spiralling out of control like a ship with no captain, and I am left wondering, ' Where are You, heavenly Father? Can You hear me in the dark?' Yet this passage tells me how much He knows me, how important I am to Him. If He has numbered my hairs, then how much more has He numbered my hands and my feet, and surely they have purpose in Him.

I am no accident, I am part of a plan, and He knows the plans He has for me.

In Psalm 139, David writes:

For You formed my inward parts;
You wove me in my mother's womb.
I will give thanks to You, for I am fearfully and wonderfully made;
Wonderful are Your works,
And my soul knows it very well.
My frame was not hidden from You,
When I was made in secret,
And skillfully wrought in the depths of the earth;
Your eyes have seen my unformed substance;
And in Your book were all written
The days that were ordained for me,
When as yet there was not one of them.

How precious also are Your thoughts to me, O God!
How vast is the sum of them!
If I should count them, they would outnumber the sand.
When I awake, I am still with You.

(Psalm 139:13–18)

There is something about this psalm that resonates in my very soul. It describes the intimacy of God's relationship with me, a relationship that began even before I knew who I was, before my consciousness took root. My soul, that secret part of me that is my link to my Creator, knows this very well, and when I am far from Him, when sin tries to come between us, then it is my soul that reaches out and cries for Him like a child missing its mother's milk:

As the deer pants for the water brooks, So my soul pants for
You ...

(Psalm 42:1)

I am fearfully and wonderfully made by Him and in Him. I am created for good works, planned by Him for me before I was born. Despite the circumstances of my birth, despite my flaws, weaknesses and imperfections, I am made for a divine purpose, and He who has numbered all the hairs of my head knows and loves me just as I am.

As the Holy Spirit reveals this to me I am reminded again to leave my Martha place. To choose to become more intentional about my everyday life, just as He is intentional for me. To remember how much He has invested in my creation, to remember the price He paid so that I could continue in His divine plan. I learn that I do not have the time to dawdle in my Martha place, I have things to do for Him, with Him. I want to become intentional in His kingdom.

I learn that to live an intentional life means setting all I do within the context of His will and purpose for me. It means seeing every opportunity that comes my way as an opportunity to further His kingdom... at work, at play, meeting people, entering into new places. It means I have a purpose shaped not by human minds or hands, not defined by my grades, my work experience or my achievements; this purpose is shaped and defined in the very heart of my heavenly Father's will. I am part of a plan, and there is one master planner

Jesus knew this, and time and time again He reiterates to His listeners:

> *By myself I can do nothing; I judge only as I hear, and my judgment is just, for I seek not to please myself but him who sent me.*

(John 5:30, NIV UK 2011)

In John 8, Jesus said:

> *When you have lifted up the Son of Man, then you will know that I am he and that I do nothing on my own but speak just what the Father has taught me.*

(John 8:28, NIV UK 2011)

> *I know that his command leads to eternal life. So whatever I say is just what the Father has told me to say.*

(John 12:50, NIV UK 2011)

As I read these passages again, I wonder if, indeed, I could I live this way? To live my life purely focused on His will? To seek not to please myself but Him who made me, who created me for His purposes? How would this change my life, my actions, my decisions, my focus, and what impact would this have on those around me?

Does it grieve His heart when I take the gifts and talents He so carefully created as part of me and use them purely in the pursuit of material gain, influence, satisfaction? I am more valuable to Him than many sparrows, not just because He loves me, but because I am part of His plan for the world. I have a contribution to make, a purpose to fulfil.

I understand now the restlessness that fills my soul, and I realise I want to become more intentional for Him. I too want to live my life to please Him, I too want to hear so clearly from my Father that I do and say what He has told me to.

To some this may suggest that life may become staid and boring, but Jesus says that He came to give life in all its abundance (see John 10:10). Scripture tells us that Jesus attended parties, drank wine, spent time with the downtrodden and the lost. He was constantly on the move. A life lived intentionally for God and in the reflection of His will is an exceptional life lived, whatever we do or don't do. Extrovert or introvert, socialite or home-body, it is the extent to which we are connected with the spirit of God that determines how abundantly we live in Him. I want to live exceptionally. I have been wonderfully and marvellously made for wonderful and marvellous things.

So I resolve to begin to examine my actions in the light of His will. I will ask myself the question, 'Why are you doing this?' more often, and if in answering I cannot demonstrate how it will please my Father then I will lay it down... and perhaps I should also ask, 'Why not?' If I know it will please Him, why am I not doing more of it?

As I go out this morning to meet a group of young people as part of a project I am starting, I choose to start my day intentionally, knowing that I am going there to do His will. As a child of God, there are no coincidences, no mistakes, no unexpected days. The Word says all the days of my life are in His hands (see Psalm 31:15). So today I will intentionally glorify His name, seek His will and do what He tells me to do.

I come to the throne room; I tell Him about my plans for the day; and I listen.

Eventide

This is a lesson I know I will need to keep revisiting. Like many Christians and particularly women, I battle constantly with a sense of inadequacy and often find myself wondering again about my purpose and whether I am where I should be or need to be. Learning again of God's intentions for me, rediscovering His purposes and His role as my Father reaffirms me and roots me again in His love. I am His and whenever I lose my way, all I need to do is reconnect to Him as my source and power. I may not find my purpose in many things but in Him it is constant and this above everything helps me to be still and know He is indeed my God.

Prayers

Father, thank you that you are intentional for me. Thank you that you have indeed numbered all the hairs on my head and that in You, I have purpose, form and function. Thank You that you made me fearfully and wonderfully and thank You that as You watched me being formed in my mother's womb, You intentionally gave me skills, attributes, gifts and form to help me achieve the purposes that I was created for. Lord, I confess there are days when I feel lost and alone, when the world does not seem to make sense and I can not figure out where and how I fit in; these are the days Lord when I retreat into my 'Martha place'. I ask Lord in Jesus name that on those days, you send your Holy Spirit to remind me that I am yours and that You are intentional for me. Open my eyes that I may see and my ears that I may hear and help me to live my life totally connected to you always. I ask in Jesus name. Amen.

For we are His workmanship, created in Christ Jesus for good works, which God prepared beforehand so that we would walk in them.

(Ephesians 2:10)

For those whom He foreknew, He also predestined to become conformed to the image of His Son, so that He would be the firstborn among many brethren; and these whom He predestined, He also

called; and these whom He called, He also justified; and these
whom He justified, He also glorified.

(Romans 8:29–30)

A s IF TO REITERATE the lessons learnt from the day before, my Father tells me I have been prepared in heavenly places, whether I understand it or not. I was made by Him for a purpose, and it does not matter if I am currently allowing myself to be used for that purpose of not, the fact is that I am what He made me.

He asks me: 'Does a chair stop being a chair because nobody is sitting on it?'

'No,' I answer, 'but Father, what if the chair does not know it is a chair?'

'Does it matter? Does that change the fact that it is a chair?' He asks.

I begin to understand; my Father made me for a purpose. The Greek word used in Ephesians is '*parakeiazo*', which means an article ready to hand, a vessel prepared for a specific purpose. I am not a random shape. I am made specifically to fit a specific purpose in His kingdom. Like a piece of Lego, I will naturally fit into the world He created around me. It is a mind-blowing thought.

In my Martha place I worry about the things that He has called me to do, the dreams and visions He has laid upon my heart. I want to do so much for my Saviour, but I worry that I am not enough, that I do not have the skills, the words, the resources to achieve all He asks of me. Yet as I look at the picture of the chair and read the words from Ephesians, I see the foolishness of my worries, of my Martha place.

He prepared all the works that lie before me and He made me perfectly to implement each one. He made all of us perfectly to implement the works because He knew what we would need to do, for it is all about Him. I realise now that I never need to go into a situation for Him worrying if I am enough, if I will 'have the right words'. I just have to understand that I am what He has made me and if I trust in His wisdom, His creation power and that He is God above all things, then I must know that I am indeed wonderfully and marvellously made. I was born ready to do His will.

I wonder what it would be like to go through life never actually fulfilling the purpose for which He made me. I would be like a chair that never got sat on, a bed that never got laid in, and it occurs to me that the knowledge of this in the afterlife, when it is too late to change anything, must be part of hell itself. I don't want to be that utensil that was never used.

In the Jesus ministry led by Stuart Lees in Christ Church Fulham, London I have learnt about 'original design', the knowledge that we each have a spiritual blueprint designed personally by our Father before creation. So I ask Him to show me my original design; to reveal to me what it is that He made me to do. What is my *shape* and what am I for? He reminds me again of the scripture in Romans 8:29–30:

- He foreknew me
- He predestined me
- He called me
- He justified me
- He has glorified me

As I read this again, it becomes clear how much divine thought has come together to put me in the very place in which I stand. He knew me, He predestined all I am, He called me, He justified me by the blood and He has glorified me. He did all of that before I was conscious enough to make any choices for myself. I am humbled and amazed. I cannot comprehend such love.

Now I understand why David says in Psalm 139:

> *How precious also are Your thoughts to me, O God!*
> *How vast is the sum of them!*
> *If I should count them, they would outnumber the sand.*

(Psalm 139:17–18)

For a brief moment I get a glimpse of how my heavenly Father feels when I doubt myself and question if I am 'good enough'. I am not just putting myself down but rather I am casting a slur on my Creator's workmanship.

When I say, 'Am I good enough?' I am actually asking, 'Did He create me properly?'

When I ask, 'Do I have the right skills, words and resources to do this?' I am actually asking, 'Is His workmanship good enough to stand up to this?'

My heart repents before Him and I promise not to ask this question again. I am well and truly made. I think about the dreams and visions He has laid on my heart. Of starting a ministry, of writing a book, and I know now there is no more time to lose and no reason to wait. I am ready; I was born ready. I was ready before I was born. I am His and I am wonderfully and marvellously made to fulfil wonderful and marvellous purposes in Jesus Christ my King.

Prepared to Run

In Hebrews 12 the bible says:

> *Therefore, since we have so great a cloud of witnesses surrounding us, let us also lay aside every encumbrance and the sin which so easily entangles us, and let us run with endurance the race that is set before us, fixing our eyes on Jesus, the author and perfecter of faith, who for the joy set before Him endured the cross, despising the shame, and has sat down at the right hand of the throne of God. For consider Him who has endured such hostility by sinners against Himself, so that you will not grow weary and lose heart.*

(Hebrews 12:1–3)

As I read these familiar words alongside Ephesians 2:10, it becomes increasingly clear that my purpose is set out before me. Like an athlete at the starting line of a marathon, I am one of millions with a 'job' to do, a 'race' to run, a 'purpose' to fulfill. These works are not just about me and my justification before the Lord, but rather about His plan for the world and all of us who live in it. He created a world that was meant for good, abundance, peace and fruitfulness and in each of us fulfilling our potential we inch the world one step closer to His original design. I see myself as one of innumerable pieces across the world, seemingly random but all joined together in His perfect plan and all fitted together in one perfect repository for all pieces, irrespective of their shape – Jesus. I read again the beautiful words in Colossians:

> For by Him all things were created, both in the heavens and on earth, visible and invisible, whether thrones or dominions or rulers or authorities—all things have been created through Him and for Him. He is before all things, and in Him all things hold together. He is also head of the body, the church; and He is the beginning, the firstborn from the dead, so that He Himself will come to have first place in everything. For it was the Father's good pleasure for all the fullness to dwell in Him, and through Him to reconcile all things to Himself, having made peace through the blood of His cross; through Him, I say, whether things on earth or things in heaven.

> (Colossians 1:15–20)

I am one of many things created by Him, through Him and for Him. I am prepared in Heavenly places for a purpose and there is a race set before me, a role to perform during my time here on earth. It is a comforting thought but also one that stirs my soul and instills in me a sense of unrest. I look around and know I have no more time to lose. I have time to make up for, things to do, places to be, people to love. In the silence I can hear the encouraging cries of those who have gone before me, I am a runner, my legs were shaped for this... it is time to take off! I will not allow myself to grow weary, tired or disheartened because my Creator, He that prepared me, is a Great God and His workmanship is perfected in Him. I am drawn to the words of the Prophet Isaiah and my soul is at peace:

Do you not know? Have you not heard?
The Everlasting God, the Lord, the Creator of the ends of the
earth
Does not become weary or tired.
His understanding is inscrutable.
He gives strength to the weary,
And to him who lacks might He increases power.
Though youths grow weary and tired,
And vigorous young men stumble badly,
Yet those who wait for the Lord
Will gain new strength;
They will mount up with wings like eagles,
They will run and not get tired,
They will walk and not become weary.

(Isaiah 40:28–31)

My prayer

Dearly beloved Father, I am sorry that I have allowed myself
to question your workmanship despite what your word tells
me. I am sorry that I have underestimated how precious
your thoughts are towards me and how much you have
prepared me for what lies ahead. Lord I want to run this
race alongside my brothers and sisters, led by Your precious
Son. I know I have a purpose and that You have prepared
me. Show me my purpose Lord and fill me with strength. I
love you Father and my soul yearns only to do your will. In
Jesus' precious name I pray. Amen.

DAY 6 — And His Banner Over Me is Love

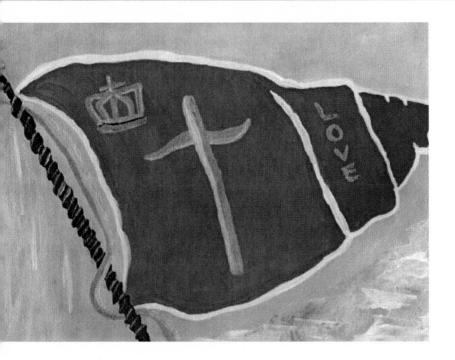

In his shade I took great delight and sat down,
And his fruit was sweet to my taste.
He has brought me to his banquet hall,
And his banner over me is love.

(Song of Solomon 2:3–4)

Today He reminds me that His banner over me is love! I am given a picture of a banqueting hall where all royalty are seated on long tables. I am seated among them although I do not understand why. Surely these are daughters and sons of Kings and I have no place here. Even as I think these words, I understand how wrong I am to think them. I too am the daughter of a King, He is the King of Kings and I am His child.

> For all who are being led by the Spirit of God, these are sons (daughters) of God. For you have not received a spirit of slavery leading to fear again, but you have received a spirit of adoption as sons by which we cry out, "Abba! Father!" The Spirit Himself testifies with our spirit that we are children of God, and if children, heirs also, heirs of God and fellow heirs with Christ, if indeed we suffer with Him so that we may also be glorified with Him.

> (Romans 8:14)

Behind each prince and princess stands a servant holding high a banner that depicts their kingdom's standards. Mine bear different signs.

I turn and look and mine is red with the sign of the cross and a crown. His banner over me is indeed love. I notice others look and see, and He tells me, 'All who see the banner over you will know that you are Mine. You belong to Me.'

I live in His kingdom, in this kingdom; Jesus Christ is the King and I am His. By His permission and grace I abide in His love. In this kingdom, in which I reside by grace alone, I am inside the vastness that is Jesus Christ. We imagine Him in His earthly form, but I have come to understand that He is so much more than anything I can comprehend or imagine and that His mercy and compassion for me is beyond all my understanding. I am drawn to the Psalmist words:

> The Lord is compassionate and gracious, Slow to anger and abounding in lovingkindness.
> He will not always strive with us, Nor will He keep His anger forever.
> He has not dealt with us according to our sins, Nor rewarded us according to our iniquities. For as high as the heavens are

above the earth, So great is His lovingkindness toward those who fear Him. As far as the east is from the west, So far has He removed our transgressions from us.
Just as a father has compassion on his children, So the Lord has compassion on those who fear Him. For He Himself knows our frame; He is mindful that we are but dust.

(Psalm 103:8-14)

As I read these verses again, I consider what it means to belong to this King, to be counted as one of His own, and I learn how foolish it is to live as if I belong to the world when I actually belong to the kingdom of an incomparable King. It is not just about how I feel inside, but also how I look to others. I am an ambassador for the kingdom; His flag flies over my house, my heart, everything I do… it is so important that I make Him proud of me with everything I do. I want people to look at me and say, 'Yes, there goes a child of God.'

Abiding in His love

What is it like to abide in His love, to sit beneath this Banner of Love, to be known as the King's own? In John 15:9–17 Jesus says:

I have loved you even as the Father has loved me. Remain in my love. When you obey my commandments, you remain in my love, just as I obey my Father's commandments and remain in his love. I have told you these things so that you will be filled with my joy. Yes, your joy will overflow! This is my commandment: Love each other in the same way I have loved you. There is no greater love than to lay down one's life for one's friends. You are my friends if you do what I command. I no longer call you slaves, because a master doesn't confide in his slaves. Now you are my friends, since I have told you everything the Father told me. You didn't choose me. I chose you. I appointed you to go and produce lasting fruit, so that the Father will give you whatever you ask for, using my name. This is my command: Love each other.

(NLT)

My eyes are opened to this place of love, abundance, peace and hope. It is such a different place from my Martha place. This is what Mary knew, as she sat at His feet, this was the place that she chose and the place I now seek to make my own.

- It is a place of joy and abundance
- *These things I have spoken to you so that My joy may be in you, and that your joy may be made full.* (John 15:11)
- It is a place where I am protected
- *… thy rod and thy staff they comfort me.* (Psalm 23:4, KJV)
- It is a place where I can bear fruit
- *I am the vine, you are the branches; he who abides in Me and I in him, he bears much fruit …* (John 15:5)
- It is a place where I can put down my burdens and find rest in Him
- *Come to Me, all who are weary and heavy-laden, and I will give you rest.* (Matthew 11:28)
- It is a place where I am refreshed with living water that slakes all thirst forever.

- *He who believes in Me, as the Scripture said, 'From his innermost being will flow rivers of living water.'* (John 7:38)
- It is a place where I am loved and accepted for who He is, not who I am!

I come to the end of the sixth day. The King loves me. He made me, He loves me, I am His and His banner over me is love, love, love!

My prayer

Dear Father, thank you that you have made me yours, thank you that I am a royal princess, crowned with your love and grace, covered by your compassion and mercy. Father, your banner of love flies over me, your abundance fills me, and as I come to this place, I am fed, watered, refreshed and I bask in the warmth of your love. How you love me Father and how amazing is it that you do! Dear Jesus help me to remember how I feel now even as I read these words of Scripture over and over again. I want to sit at your feet and remember always that I am loved by you totally and completely. Thank you Lord.

A s I come to the seventh day, I know I am changed from the inside. It is not a dramatic, mind-blowing 'Eureka!' moment. It is just a 'knowledge', and with that knowledge comes peace, joy and rest. I know I am loved. I know I walk with Him in heavenly places. I know His banner flies over me, and I know I am made for His purposes. I understand that even though I know all of these things, I still know only in part. Yet, I am content to know only in part. I trust that more will be made known as He sees fit. Most importantly, I know that I am known.

For now we see in a mirror dimly, but then face to face; now I know in part, but then I will know fully just as I also have been fully known.

(1 Corinthians 13:12)

The word used for 'known' here suggests a level of intimacy equalled only to the union between a man and a woman in marriage. He knows me perfectly and completely.

To Submit, To Surrender

Today the Holy Spirit draws my attention to the subject of surrender. This is a word that features in one of my favourite Christian songs, 'I surrender all'.[3] I am asked to think of the word and what comes to mind, and instantly I think of a white flag... it is the universal expression of surrender by, for an example, an army that recognises that it has been overcome by a more superior force. The white flag is internationally recognised as a protective sign of truce or ceasefire and a request for negotiation. The word 'surrender' itself is often defined as 'to stop resisting, to yield to an enemy or opponent'.

As I think about this, I consider that neither of these images correctly capture my relationship with my heavenly Father. I am not waving a white flag in defeat to Him, and I am not 'surrendering' to an enemy force. I am drawn to the verse in the Bible that says:

> *Submit therefore to God. Resist the devil and he will flee from you.*

> (James 4:7)

I look up the word 'submit' in my dictionary: 'Accept or yield to a superior force or to the authority or will of another person'.[4] Unlike surrender, this denotes consent and a choice, an acceptance of the superiority of the power that is submitted to.

I am made to understand why this subtle difference is important. One denotes defeat and a lack of choice, the other represents a conscious decision to defer to the authority of a more superior one. In choosing to submit to God, I am not surrendering because I have no choice and I am afraid of defeat, I am choosing to submit because I acknowledge that He is God, He is above all things and I

---

3   Judson W. Van DeVenter, 1855–1939.

4   Oxford Dictionaries Online.

consent to be under His authority in love and adoration for who He is. God wants people to submit to Him through choice and love, not surrender through fear. That is the immeasurable capacity within which He loves us, a love that allows us to choose to abide in Him, to choose His love above every other.

Likewise, I understand I am instructed not to fear the devil; I am to make a conscious decision to resist him, knowing that in doing so and choosing to submit to God, the devil has no choice but to flee from me. I learn that understanding this subtle distinction is an important part of my relationship with my heavenly Father.

Each day, I can choose to make a conscious decision to choose to submit my life, my actions, my thoughts, all that I am to Him, accepting and yielding to His spirit that is within me. In making that choice I allow myself to be controlled by the Spirit of God (Romans 8:9) and I live in Him. I can also choose to dwell in a place of sorrow, regret and inadequacy. He has given me free will, he has given me the Law and most importantly, He gave me Jesus Christ to show me the power of free will existing within His will. My choices are clear.

To Obey

I am reminded how Jesus' attitude demonstrated complete obedience and submission to God and what I can learn from Him. In Philippians 2, Paul says

> *"Have this attitude in yourselves which was also in Christ Jesus, who, although He existed in the form of God, did not regard equality with God a thing to be grasped, but emptied Himself, taking the form of a bond-servant, and being made in the likeness of men. Being found in appearance as a man, He humbled Himself by becoming obedient to the point of death, even death on a cross.*

Jesus emptied Himself and I learn that to come into a place of total communion with my Father, I too must learn to empty myself of the things I have held on to and submit myself in obedience and humility to His control. This does not leave me empty of all will but rather fills me with the power to live in the heavenly places, to make choices that are in tune with His commandments and to live in a place of trust and faith knowing that He is my provider in all things. It is a covenant set out by Jesus to his disciples:

> *Jesus answered and said to him, "If anyone loves Me, he will keep My word; and My Father will love him, and We will come to him and make Our abode with him. He who does not love Me does not keep My words; and the word which you hear is not Mine, but the Father's who sent Me.*

> (John 14:23–25)

And even more importantly, He says in John 15:

> *If you keep My commandments, you will abide in My love; just as I have kept My Father's commandments and abide in His love. These things I have spoken to you so that My joy may be in you, and that your joy may be made full.*

> (John 15:10–11)

Slowly but surely it becomes clear, if living in my 'Martha place' is by itself a very act of disobedience, how can His spirit live within me and how can I abide in his love? Each time I choose to live under the shadow of fear, stress, worry and strife, I am choosing disobedience, I am refusing to submit to His spirit within me and even worse, I am ceasing to resist the devil and naturally he stops fleeing from me. I am not alone in my 'Martha place', my Lord is absent, but I am not alone!

Submitting to the law

As I learn about the importance of obedience and submission in my relationship with my Father, I am brought to understanding about the law. Paul sets this out clearly in Romans 8 and the words of this chapter finally begin to make sense to me. The law still

dominates this world in which we live, the law that defines the wages of sin as death, that says that death is the end and that we all reap what we sow. These are the laws of Moses given to the patriarch long ago but they were never meant to become stumbling blocks to salvation or our relationship with our heavenly Father. Often, I have been driven to my 'Martha place' through guilt and shame arising because of a perceived or very real failure to keep a commandment, or to be a 'proper Christian'. I have allowed my inner critic or the perceived criticism of others to fill me with self-condemnation and drive me from the presence of a loving Father. The Spirit draws me again gently to the words of Paul in Romans 8:1:

> *Therefore there is now no condemnation for those who are in Christ Jesus. For the law of the Spirit of life in Christ Jesus has set you free from the law of sin and of death.*

The Law still exists; Jesus said very clearly that He did not come to abolish the law (Matthew 5:17) but to fulfill it, and therein lies my freedom. It is true that I will always have a natural sinful nature within me and inevitably I will break laws and commandments, but with the Spirit of Christ within me comes forgiveness, mercy, grace and compassion. It also brings the realisation that I do not need to be controlled by my sinful nature. My emotions and feelings may call me towards my Martha place but the spirit of love within me calls me to the feet of my Saviour, to sit in humility, obedience and submission. To be still and know that He is God.

Eventide

It is a final word of knowledge for the seventh day. I am His, I have been prepared by Him, chosen by Him, justified by Him and I am so totally and completely loved by Him. As I come before Him I know He is the light within me, He is water to my soul, life to my spirit and His is the air within me. As I come to the end I feel His power within me and I know that it is well with my soul. I was made for abundant life with Him and I cannot live in my Martha place any longer.

I am being 'Mary'. I am 'Mary', though not by name; I am becoming 'Mary' by nature. I am simply described by my Lord Jesus Christ in the book of Luke, chapter 10, verses 38 to 42 as if He were sitting right beside me, even now observing me as I walk into the awareness of who I am in Him, in my heavenly Father: '*Mary has chosen the good part, which shall not be taken away from her.*'

I have His love within me. It shall not be taken away from me.

The Days After

I wrote the first draft of this little book during the seven days in July 2015 when I walked with my Father through scriptures. There may be those who may query the theological accuracy of what I have written, so it is worth saying now that I do not write from any level of theological expertise neither have I sought to challenge any doctrine. My journey is based in Scripture and it is important to me that everything I have written is based in Scripture.

I have shared it because I believe that there are others like me, on a journey of discovery, and like a shared map of favourite walks, it is meant to act simply as a guide. I believe that the Holy Spirit will lead each person down their own special path. We each only have to ask in faith. He is a patient teacher, a generous and priceless gift from our Father and His wonderful Son.

In the days and weeks that have followed, I have felt the pull back to my 'Martha place'. I have found myself worrying again but, armed with the knowledge and truth of His love for me and the power of His words, I have fought my way out, I have kept my eyes fixed on Him, and am running the race He has set before me. I am getting stronger, faster, and my visits back to my Martha place are getting fewer. Its walls are crumbling and now it feels unfamiliar and strange; soon, I know, in faith, it will be just dust, and in its space will stand the new place in which I now reside – my shelter, my refuge, my strong tower.

It is a beautiful place and He lives there with me… my Father and His Son, the Prince of Peace Himself, abide there with me, and I am made glad.

A Little Bit Extra

In 2014, I wrote this story as a bit of an experiment. I had become, and still am fascinated by, the parables Jesus told and what they meant. I spent quite a lot of time imagining the scenarios in my head, and this particular story came to me on a day when I recognised myself in the story of the lost sheep. I realised that it was not that the shepherd had 'lost' the sheep in question, but rather that it had strayed, and as I thought about it some more, I wondered about it, why and how it got left behind, and this story was born.

I hope you enjoy it!

The Sheep That Stayed Behind: A Jesus Tale

He had had enough. He may be a sheep, but he knew he wasn't stupid. He had had enough of the Shepherd-Prince telling him where he couldn't go, what he shouldn't do. The warnings, the talks, it was all too much. As he surveyed the mountains and fields, he felt as if his heart would burst within him. There was so much to do and see, so much freedom out there, and he wanted it, needed it, now!

He could smell it, taste it. The wind seemed to whisper to him, soft beguiling words that told of exciting lands, tastes, adventures, opportunities, things that he was missing out on. Well, it had to stop, he thought silently, as he eyed the other sheep nestling contentedly beside the Shepherd-Prince. He would not listen anymore! He would not listen to the shepherd, he would not listen to his friends; he needed to be able to make up his own mind, define his own path. He wanted more than this – so much more.

He knew he belonged to the shepherd. He and the other ninety-nine had been handpicked by the Shepherd-King and given to his Shepherd-Prince as a gift. They had been chosen before they were born; they were his before they took their first breath. Somehow the king had known which ones to choose and which ones to leave behind. He had cast his eyes gently across each flock and pointed out the pregnant ewes to his servants, while referring to a book on his lap:

> *My frame was not hidden from you … when I was woven together in the depths of the earth. Your eyes saw my unformed body; all the days ordained for me were written in your book before one of them came to be.*

> (Psalm 139:15–16, NIV UK 2011)

He was one of the 'lucky ones' but he didn't feel lucky. He felt restrained, closeted, suffocated, not lucky. He wanted more. He couldn't understand why none of the others seemed to feel this way, why they seemed happy and content when his heart wanted to burst within him.

Each day the Shepherd Prince brought them to this same mountain. Each morning he and the ninety-nine others followed him out, dutifully responding to his morning call. They walked till they got to this mountainside, and here they grazed under his watchful eye. Here he played with them, fed them, watered them, prepared them. The sheep wasn't sure what he was being prepared for; for all he knew, it was just for the butcher's knife, but you wouldn't think it, given the gentleness with which this shepherd tended them. They always had more than enough to eat, even in the drought. Somehow, as long as they followed him, they still seemed to have enough.

He had seen the other shepherds returning home with their sheep lean and hungry, and true, he had been grateful that he was one of the chosen, but despite this, he yearned for more. He knew there was more. If he was special then surely that meant he could do more, be more? Surely he should be free to be... special! Who was this shepherd to tell him where to go? He had to get away, he needed to get away.

The plan, when it came to him, was almost as if someone had whispered it in his ear. Like a seed borne in the wind, it dropped, buried itself and began to grow. He would run away and he knew just how to make it happen.

Each evening as the sun began to drop in the western sky, the Shepherd Prince would get up and begin to gently call – he never shouted, just gently called. Each evening, his sheep would raise their heads, stop whatever they were doing and respond. They knew his voice; it was unmistakable...

My sheep hear My voice, and I know them, and they follow Me ...

(John 10:27)

Once they were all gathered, he would turn towards home and lead them. It was a long way home and sometimes they would tire, but he always seemed to lead them through the greenest of fields, by the clearest rivers.

The LORD is my shepherd, I shall not want. ... He leads me beside quiet waters.
He restores my soul ...

(Psalm 23:1–3)

Sometimes, one of them, would be so tired, they would stumble. When that happened, his gentle arms would reach down and lift the weak one onto his powerful shoulders. His shoulders seemed impossibly strong, his arms impossibly wide. This sheep had never needed such help and if truth be told, he despised those who did.

Weakness was laughable, he felt; he would never let himself be carried like a sack of wheat. That was for the old, the infirm, but not him. He was strong; he didn't need the shepherd or anyone else to help him get along.

Sometimes he would catch the shepherd watching him, his eyes gentle and sad. He knew that recently he had set himself apart. He would not join in with any of the games on the mountainside; he was tired of mindless frolicking. He didn't want to nestle in the shepherd's arms – that was for the lambs. No, he just wanted to be free.

So the idea took root and grew, and when the opportunity came, it almost seemed too simple. The day had been like any other; the long walk to the mountainside, the shepherd's gentle call, the tedious time spent with the other sheep, eating, sleeping, searching for green grass, the mindless conversation of the others. Once or twice he thought he had seen the shepherd looking at him, a gentle enquiring gaze that seemed to look right inside him, almost as if he knew exactly what he was thinking. He had looked away quickly, afraid that if he held his gaze, the shepherd would see how he really felt, see the discontent he tried so hard to hide.

That evening, as the shepherd called, he hid behind a rock on the south side of the mountain. He watched him turn towards home, saw the others follow, but he stayed. He saw his friends look back enquiringly at him, but he ignored their beseeching eyes and drew even further back. Soon the shepherd's voice was a distant murmur, soon even the bells round the necks of the other sheep were silent and he was alone!

As he emerged from behind the rock, his heart leapt in joy – he had done it, he had escaped. He leapt in the air and bleated so loudly a flock of birds jumped, startled, into the air, cawing loudly at him. It didn't matter, he was free. He raced around the mountainside bleating loudly almost giddy with the freedom he suddenly felt. As he frolicked, his eyes were drawn to the mountain and he decided to climb up the rock face. He had always wanted to do this, but each time he had tried, the shepherd had called him back. This time there was no one here to stop him. Several times he nearly lost his footing and when he got to the top, his once-white coat was dusty and snagged, but oh, the sense of exhilaration at his achievement! He had made it to the top and his chest filled with pride. He had done this all by himself. He didn't need a shepherd, didn't need anyone telling him what to do, where to go…

Once he got back down, he knew there was something else he had to do; it came to him on the wind. He actually heard it calling. There was a stream that the shepherd would never let them drink at. He had simply said it was bad, but what did that mean? It didn't look 'bad', the sheep thought, in fact it looked quite the opposite. It glinted in the moonlight as it glided smoothly over the rocks down the mountain, silently lapping at the grass. It was so clear the sheep could see his reflection in it.

Once, the shepherd had caught him looking yearningly into its depths and he had reprimanded him, firmly but clearly. 'You can drink from any stream, any puddle, any well, but not this one, never this one.'

'But why?' he had asked. 'Why not?'

'Trust me, little sheep,' the shepherd answered. 'Trust me and stay away.'

That was then, but now he was on his own, he was thirsty, and the waters seemed so inviting, so very cool.

He dipped his head. The water was indeed cool. He drank deeply, marvelling at how every fibre of his being seemed to come alive as it coursed through him.

'Ah,' he said. Oh, how the Shepherd-Prince had lied. What kind of shepherd stood in the way of his sheep enjoying these mysteries, these feelings? Surely one who just wanted to keep his 'special' sheep as 'simple sheep', unable to reason or think for themselves. Well, the others might need a shepherd, but he didn't. He was powerful; he had climbed the mountain, drank from the forbidden stream – he could do all things.

As he stumbled away from the stream, he felt strangely drowsy. His stomach seemed full in a slightly unpleasant way and he belched loudly. In the distance, he saw a tree, its leaves and branches forming a cool canopy and protection from the wind. He lay down beneath it, promising himself he would rest his eyes for just a few minutes.

When he opened his eyes again, it was dark, and he felt uneasy. His mouth had an odd and unpleasant aftertaste and his wool felt sticky. He could smell something rank and stale and worse still, it seemed to be emanating from him. He rose unsteadily to his feet and gasped in dismay. What had happened to his coat? His once full and luxurious fleece, the very one the shepherd had gently removed the tangles from with his bare hands, was now knotted and matted. The water from the stream that had appeared to be so cooling, so inviting, had formed a jelly-like residue that seemed to stick all over him, making movement difficult. His stomach felt bloated and queasy, and the smell... that smell made him gag, and it was coming from him. He bleated plaintively. He was beginning to wish he hadn't stayed behind. It was getting darker. The wind that earlier on had seemed to gently caress him as he frolicked now seemed to tug and push him while moaning in a manner that was eerie and strange.

Suddenly, he heard something that made his blood run cold. It seemed awfully close and a tremor shot through him. He had heard it before, but the last time he had been safe in his pen with the other sheep. 'Wolf!' some of the older ones had whispered reverentially, fearfully. 'Bad... bad wolf!'

They had never seen a wolf, but he knew what they were – rabid animals that hunted and ripped sheep to bits, drank their blood and left nothing of them; enemies of the shepherd folk that seemed to desire nothing else but to kill and destroy flocks, leaving trails of destruction in their wake. The shepherds had tried to placate them, to provide enough for them so they could leave the flock alone, but whatever they were given, it was never enough. It was as if their desire to destroy the flock that the Shepherd King had accumulated had a malignant life of its own that defied all rhyme or reason. When their howls had rent the air, some of the younger sheep had begun to cry but just then, the shepherd had appeared in the entrance to the pen, his face gentle in the light of the lamp he held high.

'Do not be afraid, little sheep …'

> Whoever dwells in the shelter of the Most High
> will rest in the shadow of the Almighty.
> I will say of the LORD, 'He is my refuge and my fortress,
> my God, in whom I trust.'
> Surely he will save you
> from the fowler's snare
> and from the deadly pestilence.
> He will cover you with his feathers,
> and under his wings you will find refuge;
> his faithfulness will be your shield and rampart.
> You will not fear the terror of night,
> nor the arrow that flies by day,
> nor the pestilence that stalks in the darkness,
> nor the plague that destroys at midday.
> A thousand may fall at your side,
> ten thousand at your right hand,
> but it will not come near you.
>
> (Psalm 91:1–7, NIV UK 2011)

The shepherd had sat down among them in the pen, soothed them and comforted them, his voice melodious and gentle in the dark.

'Do not be afraid, little ones, the wolves are fierce but my father and I have defeated many of them. I am here always. They will never win.'

In the end the Shepherd-Prince had fallen asleep among them, the smaller sheep nestled all around him as they slept. The howls of the wolves had gone on, but somehow with him there they seemed to fade into the distance, and the more they snuggled up to him, the more the howls and bays of the rabid creatures had seemed empty and far away.

But out here on his own, who would protect him? The Shepherd-Prince was far away, with the other ninety-nine who had listened to him, who had followed him when he called. He probably had not even noticed that one was missing, and who could blame him? The sheep knew he was alone, abandoned by his own pride, and now he would pay the price. There would be no salvation for him, no gentle hand of the shepherd to soothe him, no comforting warmth. A sob of pure desperation escaped from him.

Wolves smelt out their pray... and they could smell him – anything out there could smell him, he imagined. He knew they could; their cries had changed as they had picked up his scent. They had become excited, inflamed, and their maniacal howls made him begin to tremble uncontrollably with fear. He could hear they were getting closer, so much closer.

In desperation, he raced to the mountainside; the very one the shepherd had warned him about; the one he had been so proud earlier on about climbing. Now it seemed his only hope. Perhaps the wolves would struggle to climb it too. He could feel his heart beating as he began to climb; the sound filled his ears, alongside the howls of the wolves and the strong winds that had suddenly appeared. The mountain was deceptive; where once it had seemed welcoming and accessible, now it seemed hostile and bleak. The wind that had once seemed so friendly tore at him now. Sharp stones stuck between his hooves and ripped into his flesh, and the thorny bushes tugged at his wool, as if trying to grasp him. The higher he tried to climb, the more everything seemed to conspire to hold him back, and though he was doing all he could, he knew he wasn't getting very far. Behind him, the voices of the wolves grew louder, fiercer and hungrier. They seemed to be coming from all around him now, and he could no longer make out if they were howls, jeers or homicidal laughter. Despair wrapped its tentacles around him and his heart sank.

He knew now he would never get away. He was trapped; he would die on this mountain, torn to pieces by the wolves. It was his fault. He had thought he knew better, he had thought the shepherd was wrong, he had thought this was freedom. He longed now for the company of the other sheep, the gentle hands of the shepherd, the safety of the pen. Suddenly it all became clear, why the shepherd never let them stay out here past sunset – why he herded them home – but it was too late now; too late.

He stumbled and his hoof caught in a crack between two rocks. He pulled but it was no use. Now, he was stuck as well. He began to bleat, to cry, knowing even as he did so that the wolves would descend. It was over… he closed his eyes and waited for the jaws of death to tear into him. Then suddenly, impossibly, he felt a strong pair of hands upon him. He was lifted up and placed across an equally strong set of shoulders, and he was being carried swiftly through the night. Behind him he heard howls of frustration, strangled yelps and cries. He closed his eyes tightly, unable to believe what was happening, unable to accept that he was not dead, that he would live. His shepherd had come for him, he had found him in the night, he had rescued him from the darkness, from the wolves…

> When evildoers came upon me to devour my flesh …
> they stumbled and fell.

> (Psalm 27:2)

The journey home was long. Several times the Shepherd-Prince seemed to stumble, but he never stopped. He never put him down. In low tones he spoke to the sheep, telling him not to be afraid, to trust him, to believe that he would get him home. He told him how much he loved him, how worried he had been when he noticed he was missing. How he had searched for him everywhere until he heard him cry out.

The sheep didn't say a word; he couldn't. All he could do was listen to the shepherd's voice and marvel that he had ever doubted him. He vaguely thought the shepherd must have been hot from his efforts, because he could feel the moisture seeping through his clothes to his fleece, but even that comforted him and he nestled closer.

When they reached the outskirts of the camp where the king and his shepherd son lived with the others, the sun was beginning to awaken in the purple-bathed sky. The other shepherds were stirring, yielding uneasily to the dawn chorus of birds.

Sleep fled from them as the Shepherd-Prince cried out, 'Father, Father, I have found him... it is done!' Suddenly the camp was alive. Hands lifted him off his shepherd's shoulders and the shepherd, his shepherd, sank to the ground. It was only then that the sheep saw the price the shepherd had paid for his stubbornness.

To rescue him, the Shepherd-Prince must have waded through the wolves, fought them with his bare hands and staff. His hands and feet were torn where they had gouged them with his teeth. His side was ripped open, his face scratched and torn by thorns. The sheep stared at him, dumbfounded, in disbelief. How could this be? How could the Shepherd-Prince have carried him on his shoulders when he was so mortally wounded? How could he have braved all this, suffered all this, just for him? Why would he, when he had ninety-nine others? Why did he not just leave him to die?

> *O Lord, what am I that you care for me? This sheep that you think of me? I am like a breath, my days are like a fleeting shadow.*

> (see Psalm 144:3–4)

A sob escaped the sheep as he watched the other shepherds minister to the Shepherd-Prince. His wounds were terrible to behold, his life was ebbing away, yet his hands still reached for the sheep and he pleaded with the others to make sure he was all right, to feed him, to give him water to drink. His eyes, though racked with pain, were gentle and forgiving.

'You are one of my beloved sheep, given to me by my father, and I chose to lay down my life for yours that you may be safe, that you may live.'

Greater love hath no man than this, that a man lay down his life for his friends.

(John 15:13, KJV)

The sheep lay beside him, his heart overflowing with guilt and grief.

'Who am I, Lord, that you should care for me, that you should think of me?'

The shepherd was carried away, and the sheep knew that his disobedience and pride had cost the Shepherd-Prince His life. It was a burden too great to bear, a weight impossible to carry. What manner of man was this shepherd that He would leave ninety-nine and search for the one? That he would brave wolves and the wild to rescue one miserable sheep who had been so disobedient, who had despised his wisdom and mocked his kindness?

The sheep cowered before the king. He knew he was finished. His disobedience had cost the king his precious son! Surely he deserved to be killed? He was covered with the Shepherd-Prince's blood; amazingly, it had dissolved the jelly-like mass and his wool, though streaked with blood, was no longer matted and tangled.

He waited, head bowed, for the judgement of the Shepherd-King, for his fury... but it did not come. There was a hushed silence as he lifted his head, his eyes drawn to the steady gaze of the king.

The king's voice, when he spoke, was like his son's – gentle, ageless.

'Little sheep, I loved you and chose you to be part of my son's flock, my son loved you so much he gave his life for you. You were just a sheep but today through His sacrifice you have become more than that. You were his friend and you have been saved by His love. Go in peace, your wrongdoings are forgiven.'

Greater love has no one than this, that one lay down his life for his friends.

(John 15:13)

That evening the camp was quiet. There was no singing as the women prepared the evening meal, no whistling among the shepherds, and even the animals were silent in their pens. The disobedient sheep didn't know if all the other animals were aware of what the Shepherd-Prince had done, but he knew the news of the shepherd's death had swept through the camp like a tidal wave, sucking up all joy and happiness in its wake, leaving sadness, pain and the devastating confusion of unexpected and unexplainable loss.

The night appeared darker. It was cold. The stars, normally countless in the wilderness sky, seemed to hide their faces in shame. In the distance, all the sheep could hear the wolves baying, howling in joy as if they knew they had struck a mortal blow to the camp, that they had secured a greater prize than they had expected. Hopelessness wrapped itself around the camp like a thick cloak, and eyes stared unseeingly into the fire. Even the children were quiet.

For two days the sheep all stayed in their pen. There were no mountain walks. Occasionally someone threw in fresh hay, but otherwise there was silence, except for the muted whispering among the sheep:

'Who will love us now?'

'Who will feed us?'

'What happened? Why did he die?'

The disobedient sheep knew the answer to the third question but he kept quiet, too afraid to say what he knew, too traumatised by what he had seen to say a word. His shame sat on him like an unwelcome parasite, taunting him, eating away at him. He was inconsolable. He wanted to die.

Then, on the morning of the third day, something amazing happened. The gate to the pen was flung open and a familiar voice called. The disobedient sheep thought he was dreaming; surely he was dreaming... it couldn't be... yet, like the others, he too surged forward in joy, anticipation...

Outside the sun shone so brightly they could hardly see. The darkness had gone and it was a glorious day. Everything seemed brand new: the grass was freshly cut, flowers bloomed everywhere and the birds sang a heavenly chorus. Butterflies danced across the fields.

All this was amazing, but not as amazing as the sight before his eyes. Here, holding out scarred hands, smiling broadly, looking as if the sun itself was shining from within him, was the Shepherd-Prince.

'You are alive!' gasped the sheep.

The Shepherd-Prince looked at him, and it was a look that was unlike anything the sheep had ever seen. He felt the look, he felt the love and forgiveness in those eyes stream forth like a river of light, he felt it wash over him, through him, around him. He felt the shame dissolve, he felt the life inside him stir, unfurl and bloom under his gaze. He wondered how he had missed the beauty of the Shepherd-Prince's eyes before, he wondered how he had ever thought him boring, he wondered how he had missed the wisdom and grace that shone from him, radiant and unmistakable.

How could it be that he lived? The sheep had seen those terrible wounds; he had been covered in his blood... he knew the Shepherd-Prince had died, but here he was, somehow alive, somehow risen from the dead. The sheep stared back at him, lost in wonder, lost in joy, knowing that somehow he had a second chance to follow this prince; knowing that he, this disobedient sheep, this shamed sheep, had been forgiven. It was there in the eyes of the Shepherd-Prince. He was still loved, he was still a part of the shepherd's flock.

'Yes,' said the Shepherd-Prince as he smiled at him. 'Yes,' he said, as his wonderful gaze took in the ninety-nine others, equally amazed...

'I live.'

Lightning Source UK Ltd.
Milton Keynes UK
UKOW02f1159220316

270625UK00001B/22/P

9 781911 211106